Scholastic Children's Books,
Euston House, 24 Eversholt Street,
London NW1 1DB, UK

A division of Scholastic Ltd
London ~ New York ~ Toronto ~ Sydney ~ Auckland
Mexico City ~ New Delhi ~ Hong Kong

First published in the UK by Scholastic Ltd, 2000
This edition published by Scholastic Ltd, 2015

Text © Anita Ganeri, 2000, 2015
Illustrations © Mike Phillips, 2000, 2015

ISBN 978 1407 15760 3

Printed and bound by CPI Group (UK) Ltd, Croydon, CR0 4YY

2 4 6 8 10 9 7 5 3 1

CONTENTS

Anita Ganeri has climbed an erupting volcano, swum through shark-infested oceans and sailed round the world solo. IN HER DREAMS!

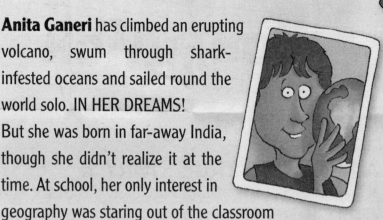

But she was born in far-away India, though she didn't realize it at the time. At school, her only interest in geography was staring out of the classroom window and working out how to escape. Since then, Horrible Geography has grown on her a bit like a mould, and she's even learned to read a map without having to turn it upside down.

Mike Phillips was born... Yippee!! No, I mean he was born in London where he grew up and up and eventually got so big he had to leave. Which is when he discovered his love of travelling, and he set off immediately to tour the world. Nearly thirty years later he has reached North Devon where he now illustrates the entire world from a sitting position.

INTRODUCTION

Geography can be shattering. But it's not the sort of shattered you feel after sitting through a double geography lesson. You know what I mean. . .

OF COURSE, ANY CLOSE INSPECTION OF THE LITHOSPHERE* WILL REVEAL THAT THE EARTH IS IN A CONSTANT STATE OF SEISMIC ACTIVITY** . . . BLAH! BLAH! BLAH!

I THINK MY BRAIN JUST BLEW A FUSE!

Z Z Z

* Lithosphere (lith-ow-sfear) is the technical term for the Earth's crust. That's the bit of the Earth that you ride your bike on. It comes from an old Greek

word for stone.

** Seismic (size-mick) is a tricky technical term for anything to do with earthquakes. It comes from an ancient Greek word meaning 'to shake'. A pretty accurate way of sizing up earthquakes, I'd say.

What on Earth is your geography teacher talking about?

Roughly translated, he's saying that you're on very shaky ground. Simple, really.

No, this sort of shattered is horribly different. Shockingly different, in fact. This sort of shattering splits the stony old Earth apart at the seams and turns people's lives upside down. So what causes this deadly devastation? An earth-shattering earthquake, that's what. And it makes double geography look like the best fun you've had in years.

The closest you'll ever get to an awesome earthquake is reading this book. YOU HOPE. But if you want to know what an earthquake might feel like, picture this scene…

One minute, you're snugly tucked up in bed, snoring and fast asleep. The next, your room starts shaking violently. Suddenly, you're flung out of bed and land with a crash on the floor. Shakily, you open one eye, then the other eye. It's chaos. There are books and clothes and mess everywhere.

7

It feels like your world's fallen apart. And what on Earth is that terrible wailing sound? No wonder you're a quivering wreck. DON'T PANIC. Your house hasn't really been hit by an earthquake. It's just your mum stomping up stairs to drag you out of bed. (And she's yelling at you to tidy your room. Again.) It's a terrifying experience, I know, but you'll soon get over the shock.

And that's what this book is all about. Strong enough to shake a city to the ground in just a few seconds, deadly enough to smash the Earth apart, and more devastating than a nuclear bomb, earthquakes are the most shattering forces of nature ever. In Earth-shattering Earthquakes, you can...

• find out how on Earth earthquakes happen.
• learn how to spot the shocking warning signs.

• build a quake-proof skyscraper that won't fall down.
• try to predict a tremor with Sid, a seismologist* (size-moll-oh-gist).

*That's a scientist who studies earthquakes. If you want to shake things up a bit, stick with me!

This is geography like never before. And it'll have you quaking in your boots.

10

A SHOCKING TRUE STORY

It was early in the morning on Wednesday, 18 April 1906. The city of San Francisco, the Pride of the West, lay slumbering in the darkness. Soon dawn would break over the sleeping city and the morning mist would give way to another beautiful day. Soon San Francisco would transform itself into a bustling city of around 400,000 people, going to school and work. But for now, most people's curtains and blinds were still drawn. Some early risers were beginning to stir. Cable car drivers, factory workers and dockers on the early shift yawned, stretched and rubbed the sleep from their eyes. Time to get up and get ready for work. Just like any other day.

And then all hell broke loose. . .

At 5.13 a.m., without any warning at all, the earth beneath San Francisco gave a sudden, sickening lurch. For 40 earth-shattering seconds, the Earth shook the city to its core. Then there was a ten second pause, followed by another massive shock. An angry, ominous, rumbling roar rose menacingly from the ground. Then the city was plunged into chaos.

It was early morning. The streets were deserted, apart from the milkmen on their rounds, and a policeman on his beat. Police Sergeant Jesse Cook saw the earthquake tearing down the street towards him.

"The whole street was undulating," he said. "It was as if the waves of the ocean were coming towards me, and billowing as they came."

Elsewhere in the city, the famous Italian opera singer, Enrico Caruso, was staying at the luxurious Palace Hotel, after a sell-out performance in the city's Opera House the evening before.

"Everything in the room was going round and

13

round," he said, later. "The chandelier was trying to touch the ceiling and the chairs were all chasing each other. Crash! Crash! Crash! It was a terrible scene. Everywhere the walls were falling and clouds of dust were rising. My God, I thought it would never stop!"

Across the city, the shock sent buildings "reeling and tumbling like playthings." Glass and windows shattered into thousands of pieces. Pictures tumbled from cracked walls. Roadways buckled and heaved. Eerily, all the church bells in the city began to ring out at once. It sounded, one witness said, like the end of the world. Terrified people, shaken screaming from their beds, rushed into the streets, still in their nightwear. In their rush, they grabbed whatever they could. Some carried pet parrots or canaries, squawking in their cages. One man was seen wearing three hats. They were all he could find. Another man clung to a coal scuttle as though it was the most precious thing in the world. Other people wandered through the streets, or sat silently on the pavements. They were too shocked to cry, or even speak. No one could believe what had happened. They had never seen such devastation before. Not surprisingly. For that April morning San

Francisco was struck by one of the deadliest earthquakes ever known.

As the rumbling stopped and the earth became still again, people tried to take stock. A heart-breaking sight met their eyes. Whole districts of the city had simply collapsed, or sunk into the ground. Almost every building in the downtown part of the city had been destroyed. Hundreds of people had been crushed to death under the falling rubble, and many more were badly injured. Some could be heard crying out from the shattered ruins. Then, just as it seemed things couldn't get any worse, things got worse. It was about 10 a.m., five hours after the first terrible tremor. Thinking the worst was over, a woman started cooking ham and eggs for breakfast. She lit a match and threw it on to the fire. Then she watched in horror. . . The chimney had been damaged by the shaking and the fire set the roof of the kitchen alight.

Within seconds, the whole wooden house had gone up in flames. The flames spread like wildfire to the rest of the block, then to the rest of the city. Unless something could be done, and fast, San Francisco would

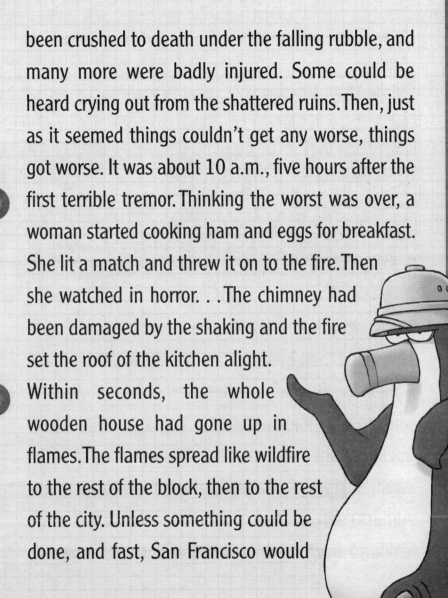

burn to the ground.

The city's brave firefighters rushed to the scene. They fixed their hoses to the nearest water pipe and waited for the water to flow. A thin trickle of water spurted out, then nothing. . . What on Earth was going on? Then they made a dreadful discovery. The earthquake had shattered the city's water mains and 300 million litres of water was slowly but surely leaking away, into the ground. With no water to use, the firefighters were helpless to put out the fire. All they could do was watch as the city went up in flames. San Francisco was doomed.

From their makeshift camps in the hills, thousands of people who'd escaped from the city also watched it burn. One shell-shocked eyewitness later wrote:

A sea of liquid fire lay beneath us. The sky above us seemed to burn at white heat, deepening into gold and orange and spreading into a fierce glare. The smoke had gathered into one gigantic cloud that hung motionless, sharply outlined against a vast field of exquisite starry blue... As night fell, it grew cold, and men and women walked up and down between the lines of sleepers, stretching their stiff limbs. Eyes, bloodshot from weariness and the pain from the constant rain of cinders, tried to turn away from the fire, but it held them in a dreadful fascination.

Fanned by fierce winds, the fateful fire blazed for three days and two nights. Then, on Saturday night, 21 April, at long, long last, it began to rain. Just in time. Next morning, the air was clear apart from dozens of wispy plumes of smoke rising from the smouldering ruins. All that was left of block after block of houses was charred, black remains. The city was unrecognizable. What buildings were still left standing were ghostly, burned-out shells. Old San Francisco had gone for ever.

EARTH-SHATTERING FACT FILE

LOCATION: San Francisco, USA
DATE: 18 April 1906
TIME: 5.13 a.m.
LENGTH OF SHOCK: 65 seconds
MAGNITUDE*: 7.9
DEATHS: 3,000
THE SHOCKING FACTS:

- The quake was the deadliest ever to strike the USA. Two thirds of the city was wiped out. Some 28,000 buildings were destroyed including 80 churches and 30 schools. About 225,000 people were left homeless.
- The city shook because it lay near the San Andreas Fault, a ghastly gash in the Earth's surface. An earthquake deep underground ripped the fault apart.
- San Francisco has grown so much that if such an enormous earthquake struck the city today, it could kill thousands of people and cause billions of dollars of damage.

SAN FRANCISCO
PACIFIC OCEAN
USA
CALIFORNIA
MEXICO
ATLANTIC OCEAN

*That's how seismologists like me measure the size of an earth-shattering earthquake. And this was a seriously big one. You can find out more about measuring earthquakes on page 92.

21

In the nineteenth century, San Francisco had grown from a small village into a brand-new, booming city. No wonder people were proud of their town. And even though many of them lost everything in the earthquake, they knew they could make the city great again. In just a few years, they'd rebuilt the city, bigger and better than ever before. But the danger isn't over yet. Everyone in San Francisco knows only too well that they're living on very shaky ground. Another earthquake could strike anytime. The trouble is no one knows when. But what on Earth makes the seemingly rock-solid ground split apart at the seams? Where does the shocking force come from that can smash a city to smithereens? Forget the nice, tame bits of nature like pretty spring flowers and babbling brooks. This is geography at its wildest. And it's happening right beneath your feet. . . Are you ready to take the strain?

CRACKING UP

As the shell-shocked people of San Francisco found out, earthquakes are horribly unpredictable. You never know when one's about to strike next. The trouble is shaky quakes usually happen deep underground so it's shockingly hard to spot any warning signs. (Your geography teacher might have eyes in the back of his head but I bet even he can't see through solid rock.) For centuries, earthquakes were so mysterious that people made up stories about them to make sense of what was going on. . .

Shocking earthquake theories

1 The native people of North America thought a giant tortoise held up the Earth. Every time the touchy tortoise stamped its foot, it set off a gigantic earthquake.

2 In chilly Siberia, people believed the Earth was carried along on a giant sled, driven by a god called Tuli. Trouble was the dogs pulling the sled had fleas. When the flea-bitten muts stopped to scratch, it made the Earth shudder and shake.

I THINK IT'S TIME WE ALL HAD A BATH!

3 Some people in West Africa blamed a love-sick giant. The giant held up one side of the Earth, they believed, while a huge mountain propped up the other and the giant's wife held up the sky. When the soppy giant let his side go to give his wife a hug, guess what? Yep, the Earth shook.

4 In a Central American story, four gods held up the four corners of the Earth. When the Earth got too crowded, they simply shook one corner to tip some people off.

5 People in Mozambique, Africa, thought earthquakes happened when the Earth caught cold. Then you could feel it s-s-s-shaking with a terrible fever. Aaachoo!

6 According to Japanese legend, earthquakes are caused by a giant catfish which lives on the seabed. When the catfish sleeps (you could call this a catnap, ha! ha!), the Earth is nice and still. But when the

fish wakes up and starts to wriggle, watch out. That's when you get an earthquake. (It must be a fantastically fidgety fish. Japan's one of the most earthquake-prone places on Earth.)

Could you catch a catfish out? Are you brave enough to save the world? To save the world from an earth-shattering experience, here's what you need to do.

What you need:
- a giant catfish
- a really large rock

What you do:

1 First, find your catfish. This might be easier said than done. The pesky catfish likes to bury itself up to its neck in mud, miles beneath the sea. And pack your suitcase – Japan's the best place to find this fish. Byeee!

2 Find a large (and I mean, really large) rock. You might need help with this bit. Do you know anyone crazy enough to help you catch a catfish?

3 Put the rock on the catfish's head so it's well and truly pinned to the seabed. Sounds cruel but the shaking should stop. Though you'll be faced with one angry old fish.

Notes:

If you feel weak at the knees just reading this, why not rope in a friendly god to help. The Japanese believed the gods were the only ones with enough power to keep the cranky catfish under control. It was only when the gods went on their holidays that the troublesome shaking began.

A bad case of wind

So, if you believe your legends, earthquakes are caused by a giant fish with a rock stuck on its head. Sounds like a very fishy story. What about any other crackpot theories? Well, there were plenty of those.

The Ancient Greek thinker, Aristotle (384–322 BCE), had another earth-shattering idea. He blamed earthquakes on a bad case of … wind. Yes, wind. Aristotle thought that earthquakes were caused by great gusts of wind gushing out from caves deep inside the Earth. Apparently, the caves sucked air in, heated it up, then blasted it out again. A bit like a gigantic, deafening fart. (Bet your teacher doesn't tell you this bit.)

But if fusty farts, crabby catfish and soppy giants weren't to blame, what on Earth was making the ground shake? Some religious leaders said earthquakes were God's way of punishing people for their sins. If people mended their wicked ways, the earthquakes would stop. Simple as that. (Whether or not it was true, it was a great way of making people behave better!) One old lady had other ideas. When an earthquake struck London in 1750, she thought it was caused by her servant falling out of bed.

Even horrible geographers got it wrong. In the 1760s, British geographer, John Michell, worked out (correctly) that the Earth shakes because of huge shock waves racing through the rocks. But he also thought (wrongly) that earthquakes were set off by the steam from enormous underground fires.

To tell you the truth, awful earthquakes had geographers stumped. And it might have stayed that way. Luckily, a brilliant German geographer, Alfred Wegener (1880–1930), was determined to get to the bottom of things once and for all. Even if it meant shaking things up a bit. This is his earth-shattering story. . .

Too much on his plate?

As a boy, Alfred Lothar Wegener spent much of his time staring into space. It drove his mother and father mad. They thought

33

young Alfred was wasting his time and would never amount to much. But starry-eyed Alfred proved them wrong. He left school top of the class and went off to university to study astronomy (that's the posh term for learning about outer space). So all that star-gazing turned out to be useful after all. (Why not try this as an excuse next time your teacher catches you staring out of your classroom window?)

NOT DISTURBING YOU WITH MY BORING LESSON, AM I, WATKINS?

NO, SIR. YOU JUST CARRY ON

But even outer space wasn't enough for adventurous Alfred. His other great love was the weather. The stormier, the better. In 1906, he set off for Greenland to study wind. This might not be your cup of tea but Alfred liked it so much he went back again in 1912, 1929, and in 1930. And when he wasn't travelling, he taught meteorology (that's the posh name for studying the weather) and geography at university. Oh yes, Alfred was a real clever clogs.

But even when Alfred was busy teaching, his mind kept wandering to other things. (Does this ever happen to your geography teacher?) He really wanted to find out more about how the Earth works. At night, he used to hurry home and scribble his earth-moving ideas down in a notebook. Here's what it might have looked like. . .

My (top) secret notebook by Alfred Wegener

One day in 1910...
I'm SO excited, I could burst. It's this cracking idea I've had. It's been worrying away at me for weeks. It all started, you see, when I was showing some of my students where Greenland was on a map. (Call themselves geographers!) Anyway, I suddenly noticed something very strange. Get this. The east coast of South America looked like it fitted snugly into the west coast of Africa. Just like two pieces of a giant jigsaw! But how can that be? Before I get too carried away, I'm going to tear up some newspaper and test out my idea. (I've decided not to tell anyone else about it just yet. Just in case it doesn't work.)

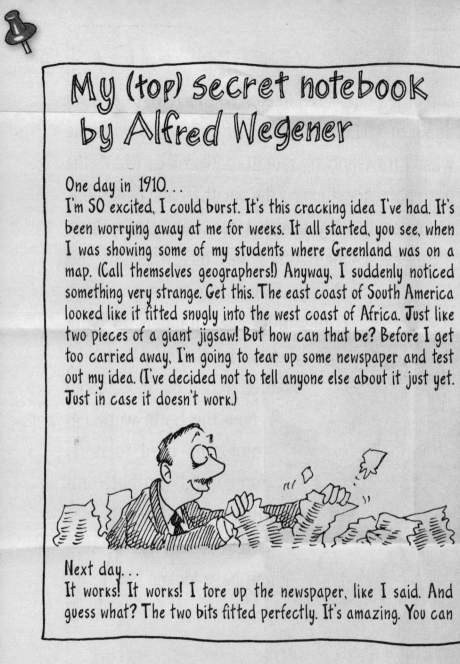

Next day...
It works! It works! I tore up the newspaper, like I said. And guess what? The two bits fitted perfectly. It's amazing. You can

hardly see the joins. But there's a very long way to go. I mean, if the two continents were once joined up, how on Earth did they drift so far apart? I really hope I can crack the problem.

Some time later...
I've done it! I really think I've done it this time! And it's ground-breaking stuff, I can tell you. This is what I think has happened. By the way, I've based my ideas on my last Greenland trip when I was watching some icebergs drifting off out to sea. Fascinating things, icebergs. But that's another story. (Sorry the sketches aren't much good.)

1 About 225 million years ago, all the continents (including Africa and South America) were one massive chunk of land. I've called it Pangaea (that's Ancient Greek for "all lands"). I reckon it was surrounded by a huge sea.

2 About 200 million years ago, Pangaea split in two...

3 Then the two big pieces split into lots of smaller bits which began, ever so slowly, to drift apart... Millions and millions

and millions of years later, these bits ended up as the continents we have today (including Africa and South America). Brilliant, eh?

Note: I'm calling my new theory "continental drift". I know it's boring but it'll do for now. Annoyingly, I still can't work out exactly what gets the continents drifting. Never mind. Perhaps it's time to check out some more lovely icebergs.

Two years later...
I've been so busy giving talks about my theory that I haven't had any time for notes. If I'd known it'd be such a shaky ride, I'd have jolly well stuck to teaching. It's been pretty depressing, actually. The problem is no one believes me. No one at all. They say I've made the whole thing up and the whole thing's just coincidence. Pah! See if I care. I'll show them I'm right. If it's the last thing I do. And what's more I can prove it. Ready?

My proof

1 Mesosaurus was an ancient reptile that lived about 300 million years ago. These days it's extinct but get this, you only find its fossils in Africa and South America. This proves that the continents were once joined up and drifted apart later. I mean, how else would you find identical reptile remains in two different places, separated by thousands of kilometres of sea?

2 It's the same with rocks. You get identical rocks in Africa and South America. They're the same age, the same type, in fact, they're a perfect match. And you don't find them anywhere else in the world. So you could say they're rock-solid proof.

3 The weather's another crucial clue. Coal formed millions of years ago. Only in warm, wet places. So Antarctica's out, you might think. Wrong! Coal's been found in icy Antarctica proving the place was once toasty warm ... and NOWHERE NEAR the

South Pole. You also get the opposite happening. Some of the rocks in Africa and South America are covered in scratches, made years ago by ancient glaciers. So you see, once upon a time, these continents were a lot closer to the South Pole than they are today.

"LET'S GO TO AFRICA" HE SAYS, "NICE AND WARM" HE SAYS...

Hah! And if that doesn't prove I'm right, once and for all, I'm going to Greenland and I'm not coming back! And that's a promise.

MAYBE JUST ONE MORE SWEATER

A very moving story

Sadly, this is exactly what happened. In 1915, Alfred wrote his ideas down in a book, called *The*

Origin of Continents and Oceans. Science was pretty stuffy then and the book caused a storm. But still nobody believed a word of it (well, it was such a boring title). Many top geologists (they're geographers who study rocks) dismissed his theory as rubbish. One of them called it "Utter, damned rot!" Another said Alfred was "taking liberties with our globe." (To tell the truth, they probably wished they'd thought up the idea themselves.) The main problem for Alfred was that he still couldn't work out what it was that made the continents drift. So he could prove things until he was blue in the face and it counted for nothing.

Bitterly disappointed, in 1930 Alfred set off for Greenland. He was never seen again…

which means he didn't live to see the day scientists finally believed his theory. For years after Alfred's death, his continental drift idea was completely forgotten. It wasn't until the 1960s that deep-sea scientists made a ground-breaking discovery that proved Alfred right. They found that some bits of the seabed are splitting apart, with red-hot runny rock oozing up through the cracks.

When it hits the cold sea water, the hot rock cools, turns hard and builds massive underwater mountains and volcanoes. In other words, the seabed is spreading. But why doesn't the Earth get bigger as the seabed spreads? Where does all the extra rock go? Scientists soon found the answer. In other places, they found, one bit of seabed is being pushed down under the other. Then the rock melts back into the Earth. And guess what? The melting exactly balances out the spreading. This means the Earth always stays the same size. The seabed and the continents are all part of a hard, rocky layer around the Earth, called the Earth's crust. If one bit moves, it shoves the rest along too, as if it's on a colossal conveyor belt. So if the seabed is moving, the continents must be moving too. Alfred had been right all along. The continents are really drifting.

What on Earth are earthquakes?

OK, you might say, but what on Earth does this have to do with earthquakes? Well, here's what else modern-day geographers have found out:

• The surface of the Earth (called the crust) is cracked into seven huge pieces called plates. (There are lots of smaller pieces, too.) Here's a helpful diagram:

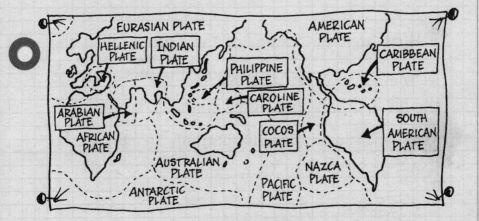

• But they're not the sort of plates you scoff your tea from. These are plates of solid rock which float on top of a layer of hot, bendy rock (called the mantle) – it's a bit like squidgy plasticine.

• Heat from the centre of the Earth (called the core) keeps the rocky plates on the move. (That's the bit that had poor Alfred stumped, remember?) You can't see all these layers from the surface. So here's an interesting X-ray view...

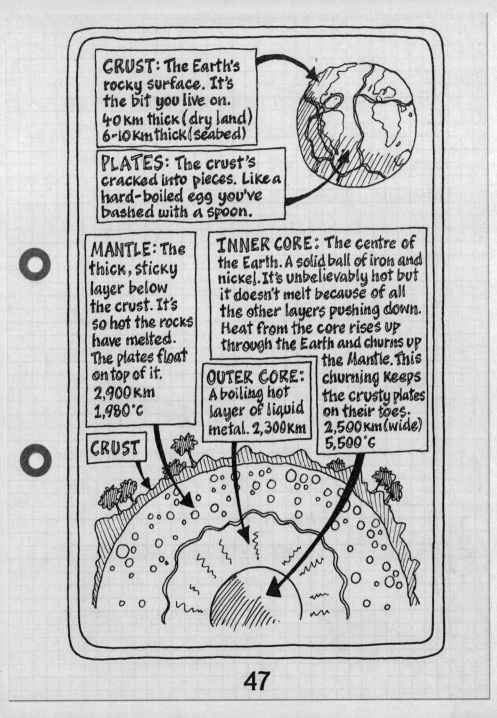

CRUST: The Earth's rocky surface. It's the bit you live on. 40 km thick (dry land) 6-10 km thick (seabed)

PLATES: The crust's cracked into pieces. Like a hard-boiled egg you've bashed with a spoon.

MANTLE: The thick, sticky layer below the crust. It's so hot the rocks have melted. The plates float on top of it. 2,900 km 1,980°C

INNER CORE: The centre of the Earth. A solid ball of iron and nickel. It's unbelievably hot but it doesn't melt because of all the other layers pushing down. Heat from the core rises up through the Earth and churns up the Mantle. This churning keeps the crusty plates on their toes. 2,500 km (wide) 5,500°C

OUTER CORE: A boiling hot layer of liquid metal. 2,300 km

CRUST

• The earth-shattering plates are always shifting, right beneath your feet. But luckily for you, they move so, so slowly, you usually can't feel a thing. Otherwise, walking to school might get very interesting. Come to think of it, you might never get there at all…

THIS MUST BE MY LUCKY DAY!

• As the plates drift along, they sometimes get in each other's way. It's a bit like being on the dodgems at the fair. As you try to barge your way past another car, you get bashed and scraped, until one of you has to give way. It's a similar thing with plates. They push and shove against each other, and get horribly jammed. (You could try this at home with two bits of sandpaper. Hold them sandy sides together and try to push them past each other with your hands. Any luck?) Over years and years, the pressure builds up and puts the rocks under serious strain. Sometime, something has to give. All of a sudden, the plates jerk apart and the ground shakes violently. And that's how you get an earth-shattering earthquake.

CAN YOU SPOT THE DIFFERENCE?

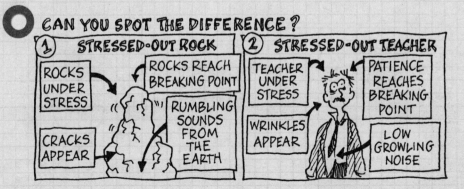

Earth-shattering fact

Thank your lucky stars you're not on the Moon. Between 1969 and 1977 seismographs (size-mow-grafs) * picked up about 3,000 moonquakes a year. Most of the quakes were caused by meteorites (they're massive great lumps of space rock) smashing into the moon's surface. And if you're wondering how on Earth you find seismographs on the moon, they were left there by moon-walking astronauts.

I'LL PUT THIS SEISMOGRAPH RIGHT HERE

WHOOOSH!

* Seismographs are posh scientific instruments for measuring earthquakes.

Quick quake quiz

Is your seismic know-how all it's cracked up to be? Is it shockingly good or horribly shaky? Why not try this quick quake quiz to find out. If you've got enough on your plate (ha! ha!), try it out on your geography teacher. It'll have her quaking with fear.

1 How many earth tremors shake the Earth each year?

a) About 100.

b) Several million.

c) About ten.

2 How long was the longest recorded earthquake?

a) Ten minutes.

b) One hour.

c) 30 seconds.

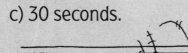

3 Where did the deadliest earthquake strike?

a) Japan.

b) China.

c) Italy.

4 How far away can you feel the shaking?

a) In the next town.

b) In the next country.

c) In the next continent.

5 How often do earthquakes shake Britain?

a) Never.

b) Not very often.

c) More often than you think.

ANSWER

1b) Believe it or not, several million earth tremors shake the Earth every year. You might just have missed one, or two. Luckily, most quakes aren't strong enough to rattle a tea cup. Only a few hundred really shake things up. And about 7-11 are truly earth-shattering.

2a) A colossal underwater quake struck in the Indian Ocean off the coast of Indonesia on 26 December 2004. It lasted for ten earth-shattering minutes – a lifetime in earthquake terms, and more than twice as long as the previous world record. Normally, even a big earthquake only lasts for a minute or less, and a small one is over in seconds so this quake really rewrote the geography books. (Read more about the effects of this monster quake on pages 123–7). The previous record-holder, a quake that struck Alaska in March 1964, lasted a measly four minutes.

WHEN'S THIS EARTHQUAKE GOING TO STOP?

3b) Unfortunately, earthquakes are often rated by numbers of lives lost. And big quakes can be big killers. Experts estimate that 830,000 people died in the quake that struck Shaanxi, China, in January 1556. Making it the deadliest quake in history. Many people lived in caves carved out of the cliffs which crumbled apart around them. The deadliest quake of recent times was the one that struck Tangshan, China, in July 1976. It reduced the city to rubble. As many as 655,000 people lost their lives. Almost 800,000 more were injured.

4c) The colossal quake that hit Lisbon, Portugal, on 1 November 1755 was the worst European earthquake ever. The shaking was felt as far away as Hamburg and even the Cape Verde Islands – a massive 2,980 km away. It lasted for several minutes, which in earthquake time is a very long shake up!

ARE YOU TREMBLING WITH LOVE, MY LITTLE BUNNYKINS?

ER... MAYBE NOT...

5c) You're most likely to experience an earthquake if you live in California or Japan (check out the next chapter to find out why). But even Britain isn't totally tremor-free. Unbelievably, Britain has up to 300 or more earthquakes a year. Luckily, most are far too faint to feel. But not all of them. In April 1884, the people of

Colchester in Essex got a nasty shock when a medium-sized earthquake shook the town, toppling several church spires and destroying 400 houses. In the villages near by, hundreds of chimney stacks tumbled down but nobody was killed. When a quake hit Shropshire in 1996 no one was hurt, but a hamster tumbled out of its cage. Poor thing!

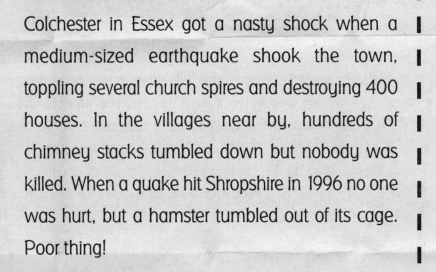

Horrible Health Warning

Earthquakes can seriously damage your health. Even though the majority of quakes pass by unnoticed, killer quakes caused more than two million deaths in the 20th century alone. DON'T PANIC. You're much more likely to be struck down by the flu. Still worried? Instead of sitting there shaking like a leaf, why not hurry along to the next earth-shattering chapter? It'll tell you where earthquakes are likely to happen so you know which places to avoid...

WHOSE FAULT IS IT?

Some places are deadlier than others. Take your geography classroom, for example. Think of all the horrors lurking behind that door. Geography books, geography tests, and worse still, geography teachers. Horrible. Now think of being on holiday. You're relaxing on a sandy beach after a dip in the warm, blue sea. (Where would you rather be?) It's the same with the stressed-out old Earth. Some places are barely bothered by earthquakes. Any tremors simply pass them by. Other places are on seriously shaky ground. A killer quake may be only seconds away. So where on Earth are these quake-prone zones?

Quick quake guide

Remember how the Earth's rocky crust is cracked into pieces called plates? Well, you'll find most of the shakiest places on Earth where two pushy plates meet up. In fact, this is how 95 per cent of all earthquakes happen. The exact type of earthquake you get depends on exactly how the plates behave. Feeling under pressure? Don't worry. Here's seismic Sid with his quick quake guide.

Hi, Sid here. Sizing up earthquakes is simple really. Once you know what you've got on your plate. Get two rock-hard plates together and something's got to give. . .

1 Pulling apart

In some places, you get two plates pulling apart. Red-hot, runny rock from the Earth's mantle oozes up to plug the gap. All that pulling sets off lots of small-ish earthquakes. Or you could call them seaquakes (well, they take place in the sea bed). Most of these quakes happen underwater, far from any land. So they're pretty harmless, unless, of course, you happen to be a fish. . .

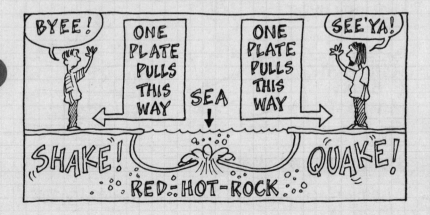

2 Going under

In some places, you get two plates crashing head-on in a colossal collision. One plate gets pushed under the other plate and its rocks melt back into the Earth. If you're planning a holiday near the coast, watch out. Slowly but surely, the seabed might be sinking under the land. Triggering off some of the worst earthquakes of all.

3 Slipping and sliding

In some places, you get two pushy plates trying to shove past each other. If they slide by nice and gently you get lots of tiny tremors. They're nothing to worry about and don't do much harm. But if one plate gives suddenly, beware. You could be in for a truly earth-shattering shock.

FAULT LINE

ONE PLATE SLIDES THIS WAY

ONE PLATE SLIDES THIS WAY

LAND

Earth-shattering fact

If you like living dangerously, why not hop in a boat and head off for the Pacific Ocean. It's lovely and warm and blue. But be careful. Deadly danger lurks in its depths. The land around the edges of the Pacific is the shakiest on Earth. This is where huge segments of seabed are sinking under the land, setting off massive earthquakes. In fact, more than 80 per cent of all earthquakes happen here. Still going?

TEACHER TEASER

If you want to give your teacher a shock, put your hand up politely and ask him or her this harmless-sounding question:

Is this a trick question?

No, it isn't. In the winter of 1811–1812, the state of Missouri, USA, was struck by three of the worst earthquakes in American history. Each quake made the Earth shake more than 1,600 km away. And if that wasn't shocking enough, the quake caused the Mississippi River to change course completely and start to flow north instead of south. No wonder the fish were worried.

The fish weren't the only ones who got a nasty shock. The quake took everyone by surprise. You see, Missouri was the last place on Earth you'd expect to get an earthquake. It's nowhere near the edge of a plate. Seismologists now reckon that about five per cent of earthquakes happen in the middle of plates, probably along cracks left by ancient earthquakes. Trouble is, they don't know where these cracks are.

Finding fault

While your geography teacher's having her teabreak, knock on the staffroom door. Make up an excuse like, "Please, Miss, I want to be a seismologist when I leave school. Do I have to be good at geography?" While she's replying, sneak a good look at the mug she's using for her tea. Is it horribly chipped and cracked? Would one good tap shatter it into pieces?

(Only try this if you want to do extra homework for the rest of your school days.)

Funnily enough, the stressed-out Earth is a bit like your teacher's old mug. How? Well, its surface is criss-crossed by millions of cracks.

The deepest cracks mark where two plates meet. Of course, horrible geographers don't call them cracks. They've thought up something much more boring. The tricky technical name is faults. But they're not the sort of faults your mum or dad mean when they tell you off for being untidy or picking your nose. These faults are weak spots in the Earth's crust, like the cracks in your teacher's mug. Pile on the pressure and these faulty rocks snap, triggering off earth-shattering earthquakes.

Geographers pick out three types of fault, depending on how the rocks move. Here are Sid's top tips for telling these fickle faults apart.

SID'S SEISMIC NOTEBOOK...

1 Normal fault. Watch out for places where two crusty plates are pulling apart. Tell-tale signs are where you see one slippery plate sliding under another.

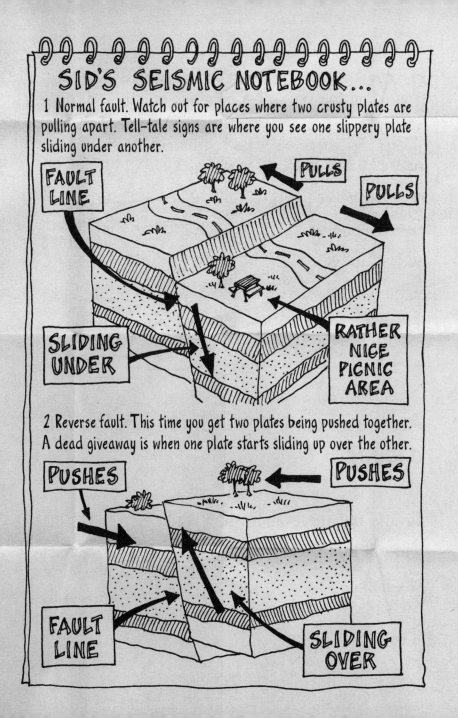

FAULT LINE

PULLS

PULLS

SLIDING UNDER

RATHER NICE PICNIC AREA

2 Reverse fault. This time you get two plates being pushed together. A dead giveaway is when one plate starts sliding up over the other.

PUSHES

PUSHES

FAULT LINE

SLIDING OVER

3 Strike-slip fault. This is where two plates are sliding past each other. One slips one way. The other slips the other way. Very slippery characters. This means that fences or roads that once matched up don't match up any more.

WHAT HAPPENED TO THE ROAD?

SLIPS

SLIPS

FAULT LINE

Are you brave enough to pick fault in a fault?

To find out more about how strike-slip faults tick, why not try this tasty experiment. Go on, it's a piece of cake.

What you need:

• A cake (for the Earth's crust). Note: The best sort of cake to use is one with lots of layers of sponge, jam and cream. They'll look like the layers of rock in the Earth's crust. And they'll taste yummy, too.

• A knife. (Be careful.)

What you do:

1 Cut two large, gooey slices of cake.

2 Press the two slices together.

3 Now pull one slice towards you and push the other away from you so they squidge by sideways. Congratulations! You've just demonstrated how a strike-slip fault works (well, almost). Simple, eh?

4 Now eat the bits of cake. Delicious!

P.S. Sick note: You can adapt this activity for the

other two types of faults, too. But don't blame me if eating all that cake makes you feel horribly sick. If you do, that's your fault.

FAULTS – THE SHOCKING FACTS

1 The most famous fault on Earth snakes across sunny California, USA. Here the Earth's literally splitting apart at the seams. This crazy crack's called the San Andreas Fault and at any time now it could shake California to the core.

2 From the air, the fault looks like a ghastly scar running across the landscape. It's about 15–20 million years old and about 1,300 kilometres long. And it's actually a system of several faults rather than a single one. No wonder California's feeling the strain. It has more than 20,000 tremors a year.

3 The fickle San Andreas Fault marks the place where the North American Plate (on the east) meets the Pacific Plate (on the west). It's a strike-slip fault (remember those?) which means the plates are sliding past each other. Actually, both plates are sliding in the same direction. But because the Pacific Plate moves much faster than the North American, it looks like they're pulling in opposite ways.

SAN FRANCISCO

PACIFIC PLATE

LOS ANGELES

NORTH AMERICAN PLATE

SAN ANDREAS FAULT

MY GRAN'S BEST PLATE

4 For most of the time, the plates slip by smoothly and trigger only tiny tremors. Creepy geographers call this creeping along. Sometimes, though, the plates get horribly jammed. The pressure builds up . . . and up . . . and up, until one plate gives way under the strain and the other plate jerks forwards.

5 You might think any sensible person would prefer to keep their feet on much firmer ground. But you'd be wrong. Horribly wrong. If mingling with famous film stars is your cup of tea, head for Los Angeles (the home of Hollywood). About 18.5 million people live in the city, perilously close to the San Andreas Fault. Another big city, San Francisco, sits practically on top of it. And, as you know, San Francisco's horribly earthquake prone. Remember the disastrous 1906 quake?

6 Seismologists say the most fragile bits of the fault are the north and south ends. They've been storing up trouble for centuries. And they could reach breaking point at any time . . . with catastrophic consequences. As they've done many times before. Time to pay a second visit to shaky San Francisco. . .

The Daily Globe

CITY REELING FROM KILLER SHOCK

The stunned residents of San Francisco are still reeling from the shock today after yesterday's massive earthquake. With a magnitude of 6.9, it was the biggest quake to hit the city since the Great Quake of 1906. Once again, San Francisco has been shocked to the core. The quake struck the city in the early evening, at the height of the rush hour. Thousands of people had already left work and were on their way home. The freeways were jammed with rush hour traffic. Pedestrians packed the pavements, chatting or stopping for a beer. At Candlestick Park, the baseball game was already in full flow. The San Francisco Giants were playing Oakland Athletics in the American Baseball

World Series. Some 62,000 fans had packed the stadium to cheer their team on. All in all, just a normal day in the life of our busy city.

Then, at 5.04 p.m., disaster struck. In the Santa Cruz mountains to the south of the city, a section of the San Andreas Fault snapped suddenly under centuries of strain.

A 40-kilometre crack ripped the Earth open. Just

SNAP TO IT

six short seconds later, the shock waves reached San Francisco. . .

For 15 seconds, the city was shaken to its core. Fifteen seconds that seemed like for ever.

Reports just reaching us put the death toll

SHAKY START

at about 63 but with thousands more people injured or missing.

All over the city, buildings have been toppled and smashed apart. A two-kilometre stretch of the freeway has snapped in two and collapsed, crushing motorists underneath. Elsewhere in the city, thousands of homes and businesses lie in ruins.

The worst-hit parts of the city are those around the bay, which were built on land reclaimed from the sea. Here houses and apartment blocks have simply sunk into the soft ground.

With the risk of after-shocks a real possibility, the city's emergency services have lost no time clearing the streets. Their advice to everyone is to go home, turn off the gas (in case of fire) and stock up on food and bottled water.

HEAD HOME

Now the terrible task of rescuing the injured from the rubble can begin in earnest.

The clean-up of the city will take many years. Rebuilding people's shattered lives will take even longer. But most San Franciscans realize they have been lucky this time. They know it could have been worse. Much worse. For some time now, seismologists have been predicting the Big One. No one knows if this was it. An even more powerful quake may be just round the corner. Despite everything, it's a risk many people are willing to take. Asked if she would now leave the city, one woman told us,

"Why should I? This is my home. Anyway, I survived the last one, didn't I? What are the chances of being in another?"

HOME SWEET HOME

Only time will tell...

EARTH-SHATTERING FACT FILE

LOCATION: San Francisco, USA
DATE: 17 October 1989
TIME: 5.04 p.m.
LENGTH OF SHOCK: 15 seconds
MAGNITUDE: 6.9
DEATHS: 63
THE SHOCKING FACTS:

• The city's major skyscrapers swayed by several metres but did not fall down. Still, the quake was horribly costly, causing almost $6 billion (£3.9 billion) of damage.

• In the year after the earthquake, more than 7,000 aftershocks were recorded around San Francisco. One that hit half an hour after the quake had a magnitude of 5.2.

• For such a big earthquake, the death toll was low. Thanks to the brilliant emergency services (fire, police and ambulance). In cities like San Francisco, the emergency services are trained to be ready and waiting when a quake strikes. An alarm sounds to give them a 20-second warning. It doesn't sound long but it's long enough to get rescuers and equipment in place, fast.

While you're still in shock, here's a warning about the next chapter. This book has got off to a very shaky start. But things are about to get worse. Feeling brave? You'll need to be as you wave goodbye to this earth-shattering chapter and crash into the next one. . .

Picture another scene. This time you're not at home in bed. You're sitting in your classroom, snatching another quick snooze. Suddenly, the Earth starts to shake. You wake up with a start. The windows are rattling, your teeth are chattering, books and pencils are flying everywhere. . . What on Earth is going on? DON'T WORRY. It might feel like you've been struck by an earthquake but thankfully you haven't. It's only your geography teacher exploding with rage.

A real-life earthquake's a million times more mind-blowing. (If you can imagine that.) And, believe it or not, all this mayhem and chaos is down to a bunch of waves. . .

What on Earth are shock waves?

Forget the waves you see rippling across the sea. The sort that give you a soaking when you're swimming or capsize your canoe. These waves aren't wet or windswept. No wonder you're confused. Time to call in Sid, our expert. . .

WHAT ON EARTH ARE THESE WAVES, THEN, IF THEY'RE NOT WET?

They're gigantic waves of energy. Don't worry, I'll explain. For years and years, strain builds up in the rocks until, one day, they go snap. Like a gigantic Christmas cracker. Then where does all that pent-up energy go? It blasts out through the surrounding rocks in gigantic, wobbly waves, that's where. You can't see this sort of wave. In fact, you can't feel them . . . until they hit the surface and give the Earth a really good shake.

WEIRD. WHAT ELSE SHOULD WE KNOW ABOUT THESE SHAKY WAVES?

Well, for a start, there are several different sorts. When they were discovered, geographers got horribly excited and gave the waves boring names. Pretty sad, eh? Want to know what the waves are called? Sure about that? OK, here goes. . .

1 Body waves. These waves travel through the Earth's insides until they reach the surface. There are two main types:

• *P waves*. These waves make the rocks squash and stretch, like a massive spring. You press the spring down, then ping! It springs back again. It's the same with the rocks. The P stands for primary because these pushy waves reach the surface first. Well, I warned you the names were boring.

- *S waves.* These waves race through the rocks in ripples, like when you hold the end of a rope and give it a good shake. The S stands for secondary because, guess what, they're the second to surface.

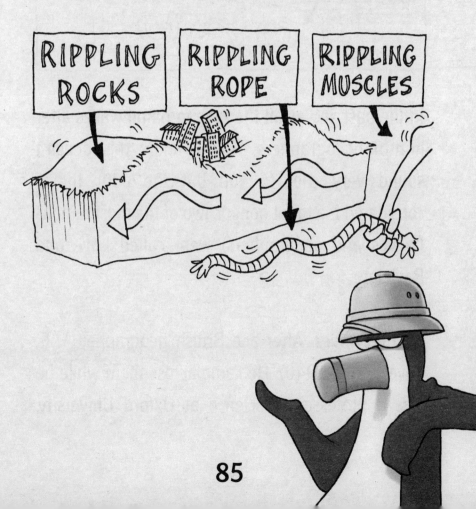

2 Surface waves. These waves shoot through the Earth's surface, shaking and rolling the ground.

In the past, it was all the rage to name waves after horrible geographers. Now I know this doesn't sound very cool to you but the poor things considered it a great honour. Two of the most famous (waves and geographers) were called Love and Rayleigh.

• *Love waves*. After ace British geographer A. E. Love (1863-1940). He came across them while he was a professor of science at Oxford University.

Love waves shift rocks from side to side.

SHIFTY ROCKS

SHIFTY PROFESSOR

• *Rayleigh waves.* After posh John Strutt, Lord Rayleigh (1842–1919). Lord Rayleigh was filthy rich and had his own private laboratory in his posh mansion. He was also a professor of physics at Cambridge University. Even though he'd been a sickly child, John was sickeningly brainy. He didn't have to go to school (how lucky can you get?). His rich dad hired a private tutor so he could do his lessons at home instead. John loved science and maths (strange but true) and he also liked travelling. In fact, he had lots of his best ideas on holiday. Amongst other things, he worked out why the sky is blue and discovered a new gas in the atmosphere. For this, he won the Nobel Prize for Physics in 1904. He also discovered a type of surface wave which moves through rocks in a rolling action.

ROLLIN' ROCKS

ROCK'N'ROLLIN' PROFESSOR

HMM. BUT HOW DID THEY KNOW WHERE THE WAVES WERE, IF THEY COULDN'T SEE THEM?
Good point. You're smarter than you look. Actually, it was a mixture of using their imaginations and being brilliant at maths. First, they tried to imagine what the insides of the Earth looked like. Then they used maths to work out where the waves would be. Sounds like horribly hard work? Lucky I've brought a picture along...

AN EARTHQUAKE: the inside story

FOCUS: The spot underground where the rocks first go snap. It's also called the hypocentre. This is where the waves start from. It can be very deep down (over 300km); medium deep (300-70km) or shallow (less than 70km).

EARTH'S CRUST

EPICENTRE: The bit of the Earth's surface directly above the earthquake's focus. The bit that usually shakes the most.

ELASTIC SHOCK WAVES: Blast upwards and outwards from the focus.

EARTH'S CORE

EARTH'S MANTLE

ARE THE DEEPEST EARTHQUAKES THE WORST?

Not necessarily. Deep quakes are stronger, it's true. But shallow quakes do more damage. Usually. This is because the waves don't have far to travel from the focus to the surface. So they don't lose power. They shake the ground horribly strongly but only a small bit of it. Deep quakes feel less shaky but cover more ground.

HOW FAR CAN THESE WAY-OUT WAVES TRAVEL?

The waves from a seriously earth-shattering earthquake can travel thousands of kilometres around the Earth. Take the quake that hit Chile in 1960. The surface waves were so strong they whizzed 20 times around the Earth and could still be felt more than two days later.

WOW! THEY MUST REALLY MOVE, THEN?

Sure do. P waves (remember them?) are the fastest. They speed along at an awesomely quick six kilometres a second in the crust. That's like travelling from London to Paris in a minute! Ear-witnesses have reported hearing a loud roar as the waves hit the surface. S waves aren't far behind, followed by slower, surface waves. But the different types of rocks they race through can make the whizzy waves speed up or slow down.

Now you're a whizz with waves, you can put them to good use. Unlike Love and Rayleigh, seismologists don't have to guess what the Earth's insides look like anymore. They use shock waves to suss out about the rocks. They also use shock waves to work out just how horribly violent an earthquake is. Read on to find out more.

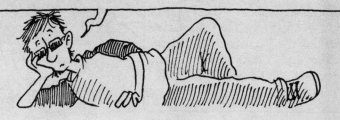

Scales of destruction

So how do you measure exactly how earth-shattering an earthquake is? It's shockingly difficult even for the experts. Why? Well, where on Earth do you start? With the earthquake's power? The damage it does? Or the size of the crack that caused it? In fact, geographers measure all three things. Which makes life horribly confusing. Here's Sid again to try to make sense of three of the handiest earthquake scales. Which one do you think works best?

A

Name: The Modified Mercalli Scale

What it measures: Earthquake intensity. This means how strongly the earthquake shakes the Earth and the damage it does. Records of earthquake intensity are great for studying ancient earthquakes. More importantly, they allow emergency services to be ready when an earthquake strikes. It's like listening to a rock band playing REALLY LOUD music. . . And they don't come much louder than the one, the only, the truly earth-shattering QUAAAKKES!

You can think of intensity as how loud the band sounds to your ears alone, no matter where you're standing in the concert hall — front, middle, back or even outside it.

THE DAMAGING DETAILS:

EARTHQUAKES ARE RATED ON A SCALE OF I (1) TO XII (12). HERE'S HOW THE SCALE WORKS...

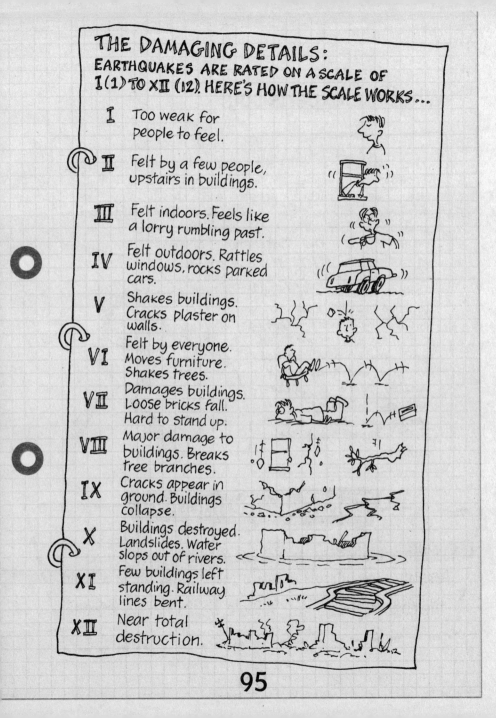

I   Too weak for people to feel.

II   Felt by a few people, upstairs in buildings.

III   Felt indoors. Feels like a lorry rumbling past.

IV   Felt outdoors. Rattles windows, rocks parked cars.

V   Shakes buildings. Cracks plaster on walls.

VI   Felt by everyone. Moves furniture. Shakes trees.

VII   Damages buildings. Loose bricks fall. Hard to stand up.

VIII   Major damage to buildings. Breaks tree branches.

IX   Cracks appear in ground. Buildings collapse.

X   Buildings destroyed. Landslides. Water slops out of rivers.

XI   Few buildings left standing. Railway lines bent.

XII   Near total destruction.

What the experts say:

This scale's a bit hit and miss, I'm afraid. Trouble is it relies on what people see and feel. Ask five different people and they'll say five different things. So, you'd have five different grades for the same earthquake. See what I mean? And the intensity changes depending on where you're standing. (So when the Quakes played "Shake, rattle 'n' roll", it sounded really loud to you because you were standing right at the front. But your mate who turned up late and was stuck outside heard a quieter version.) Besides, who wants to hang around and check out the damage?

Earth-shattering fact

You can use anything to measure intensity. Even a horse. In Australia, some people compare the shaking felt in a slight earthquake to a horse scratching its back on a fence.

B

Name: The Richter Scale

What it measures: Earthquake magnitude. This means how much energy an earthquake releases when the rocks break. (It's this energy that shoots along in seismic waves.) Remember the Quakes? Sorry, REMEMBER THE QUAKES? Imagine listening to a solo on Johnny Shake's lead guitar. Making allowances for how close you're standing to the stage. So that it sounds just as LOUD wherever you are.

The damaging details:

The Richter Scale was named after top American seismologist Charles F. Richter (1900–1985). In 1935 Charles was working at the Seismological Laboratory in quake-prone California, USA. It was a plum job for a young man. But Charles wasn't bothered about fame and fortune. No. He was utterly fed up. Fed up with answering the phone all day to boring old journalists, asking the same boring old question,

HOW BIG WAS TODAY'S QUAKE?

You see, at that time, the only way of sizing up earthquakes was with the Modified Mercalli Scale. Trouble was, you never got the same answer twice. It was hopelessly unreliable. Grumpy Charles Richter scratched his head. He had to find something better. Something that even those pesky journalists could understand. Then Charles had a brainwave. He compared the time it took for the different waves to show up on his seismograph, to figure out how far away the earthquake was. Then he measured how far and how fast the ground was shaken about by the shock waves at the place where his seismograph was. Then, making allowances for how far away and how deep the earthquake was, he calculated how powerful it was. (Phew! It's complicated.) It was much more accurate and scientific. Charles's new, improved scale looked something like this:

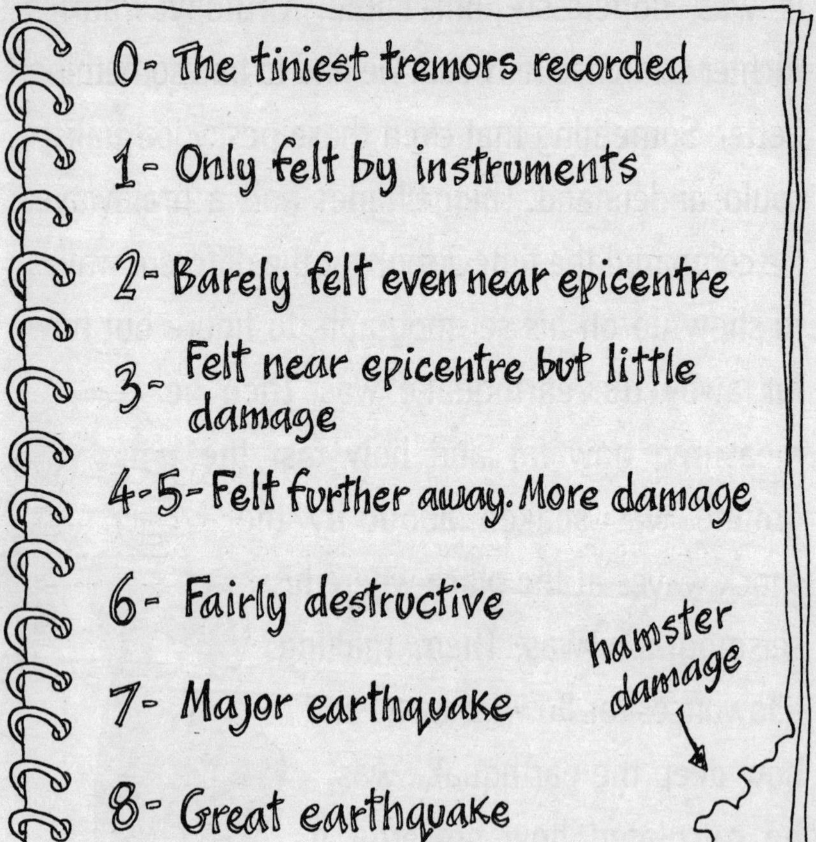

0 - The tiniest tremors recorded

1 - Only felt by instruments

2 - Barely felt even near epicentre

3 - Felt near epicentre but little damage

4-5 - Felt further away. More damage

6 - Fairly destructive

7 - Major earthquake

hamster damage ↓

8 - Great earthquake

And it doesn't stop there. Modern, ultra-sensitive seismographs can record really teeny tremors, down to −2 or −3. But don't think a magnitude 7 earthquake is only a little bit worse than a magnitude 6. On the Richter scale, each step up means a ten-fold increase. So a 7 is actually ten times bigger than a 6, but only a tenth as big as an 8. Got it?

What the experts say:

This scale's always a popular choice. It's the one they use on the telly. The only snag is it can't really cope with megaquakes. (They're the ones above 8.5)

C

Name: The Moment Magnitude Scale

What it measures: Seismic moment. This measures the total size of an earthquake. The whole shocking lot. Meanwhile, back at the Quakes concert. . . Make allowances for how far you're standing from the stage. Then take out your earplugs and it's still like listening to the whole ear-splitting band, turned up really LOUD!

The damaging details:

This scale takes everything into account, from the first crack in the rocks, to how much the Earth shakes and how long the earthquake lasts.

What the experts say:

This scale is the experts' choice. It's tricky to calculate but awesomely accurate because it gives the whole earth-shattering picture. And it's brilliant for those really big quakes, between 9 and 10. So brilliant, in fact, that some of the biggest quakes have been upgraded. The 1960 Chile megaquake measured 8.5 on the Richter scale. Pretty big, you'd think. True, but actually it was much, much bigger than that. Its moment magnitude is now rated as 9.5, making it one of the most massive quakes ever.

Killer quakes

The catastrophic Chile quake was the most powerful quake of the twentieth century. But in the worst earthquakes ever, it doesn't even make the top ten. That's because many earthquake lists are based on the numbers of people killed. It's tragic but true. In Chile's case, some 2,000 people lost their lives. Which was pretty bad. But for such a great quake, it was amazing there were so many survivors.

TOP TEN EARTHQUAKES

	LOCATION	DATE	DEATHS	MAGNITUDE
10:	Ashgabat, Turkmenistan	1948	110,000	7.3
9:	Kanto, Japa	1923	142,000	7.9
8:	Ardabil, Iran	893	150,000	Unknown
7:	Gansu, China	1920	200,000	7.8
6:	Damghan, Iran	856	200,000	Unkown
5:	Sumatra, Indonesia	2004	227,000	9.1
4:	Aleppo, Syria	1138	230,000	Unknown
3:	Haiti, Caribbean	2010	316,000	7.0
2:	Tangshan, China	1976	655,000	7.9
1:	Shaanxi, China	1556	830,000	8.0

NB: some of these earthquakes were so long ago that experts have had to estimate their magnitude. But if they were big enough to go down in history, they must have been pretty bad!

Some of these quakes happened a long time ago when there weren't any accurate records. So the numbers of deaths are based on guesswork. The true numbers might be much higher … or much lower. There's really no way of telling.

One thing's for certain. Earth-shattering earthquakes are horribly dangerous. And they can happen almost anywhere, at any time. So to be on the safe (well, safe-ish) side, surely it's best to stay away from places known to be prone to quakes? You'd think so, wouldn't you? You really would. But plenty of people would disagree…

ON VERY SHAKY GROUND

What do places like San Francisco, Los Angeles, Mexico City and Tokyo have in common? Give up? The answer is they're some of the biggest and busiest cities on Earth. And they're all built on very shaky ground. So why on Earth do people live in such horribly hazardous places? After all, a big quake could raze a big city to the ground in a matter of seconds. Amazingly, hundreds of millions of people still live in quake-prone zones. Despite the appalling dangers. If you ask them why they don't just move out and go and live somewhere safer, they'll probably reply that for most of the time they're as safe as houses at home. Besides, the worst may never happen. But then again, it just might...

Catastrophe in Kobe

Kobe is a bustling city in southern Japan. It's one of Japan's biggest ports and an important centre of industry. Unfortunately, earthquakes shake Japan regularly, though there hadn't been a big quake in Kobe for some time. Until 17 January 1995, that is. So what does it feel like when your world's shaken apart? Here's how the events of that fateful day might have appeared to a young boy.

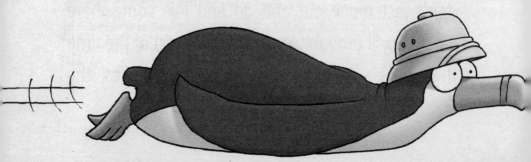

The earthquake by yoshi

We learned all about earthquakes at school. So I knew Japan got loads of them. Sometimes we did earthquake drills. But they were pretty boring. Anyway I wasn't a bit worried. Kobe's a really brilliant place. I've lived here all my life. It's really nice and safe. Besides, I didn't really believe in earthquakes, anyway. But I do now. . .

Last Tuesday, things got really scary. It was early in the morning and I was fast asleep. Next thing I knew, I was thrown out of bed on to the floor. The floor was shaking. But that wasn't all. We live in a block of flats and it wasn't just the floor shaking. The whole building was shaking. It was really scary. It was dark and I didn't know what to do. I could see things skidding across the floor. I guessed it must be my bookcase and my bed. To make matters worse, there was a terrible noise, like a monster roaring. I heard my mum calling to me and my sister. Then my dad came into my bedroom with a torch. He told me to go into the kitchen and get under the kitchen table, like we'd been taught at school.

I wish I'd taken more notice. It was hard to stand up and walk but I did what my dad said and went to the kitchen. My sister was crying and hugging my mum. You see, she's only five. I was scared too but I tried not to show it. The shaking seemed to last for ever and ever. Then, at last, it stopped. Mum and Dad held our hands tightly and we ran out of the flats into the street.

Outside, things were really bad. It was just getting light so we could see all the damage. Our building wasn't too badly hit but the block next door had toppled over and smashed to smithereens. It was the same all the way down our street. Half the houses had collapsed. It took a bit of getting used to. You think people's houses will last for ever. Some of them were my friends' houses. I really hoped they were safe. And there were these huge cracks in the pavement. Everything was ruined. One man said it was like a giant had stamped on the city and squashed it flat.

I sat on the pavement with my mum and my sister while my dad went to see if he could help. There were lots of people just sitting there, staring. My mum said it must be the shock. Anyway, I wasn't even frightened anymore. I was just sad and I was really cold. We left our house in such a rush we didn't bring our coats or anything with us. At least my mum and dad and sister are safe. Our next-door neighbour was trapped in the rubble and my dad helped pull her out. I was really proud of him. But there were lots of people shouting and crying because they couldn't find their friends and relatives. It was really horrible.

I don't know how long we waited in the street. It felt like hours. Then later that day, my dad fetched us and took us to a hall in another part of the city which wasn't so badly damaged. The hall belongs to the steel company my dad works for. Dad says his company will look after us for the time being. We

can't go home because there's no water or gas or electricity, and our house isn't safe. The hall's really noisy and crowded because there are lots of other families here.

But a man came and gave us some warm blankets and food. It was only rice-balls to eat but I was so hungry I didn't care. And it stopped my sister crying. Mum said that other people were staying in schools or shrines. And that all of us were the lucky ones. I'm glad we didn't have to stay in my school.

It's OK here and I've made some new friends but I don't know how long we'll be staying. Still, Dad says I must put a brave face on it and look after my little sister. I told him I'll try. But it isn't easy. Especially as Dad thinks we might be in for some aftershocks. They're little shocks after the big earthquake. I really, really hope he's wrong. I don't want to have anything to do with an earthquake ever again. I just want to go home.

EARTH-SHATTERING FACT FILE

DATE: 17 January 1995
LOCATION: Kobe, Japan
TIME: 5.46 a.m.
LENGTH OF SHOCK: 20 seconds
MAGNITUDE: 7.2
DEATHS: 4,500; 15,000 injured
THE SHOCKING FACTS:

• The quake caused massive destruction. Some 190,000 buildings were damaged even though many were meant to be earthquake-proof. Fire burned thousands more buildings down.

• The Hanshin Expressway, the raised main road linking Kobe to Osaka, keeled over on its side. Because it was early morning, the road was almost deserted. A few hours later and it would have been packed with cars.

• If Kobe wasn't bad enough, an even deadlier magnitude 8.9 quake hit Japan in March 2011. The quake happened underwater, triggering a devastating tsunami.

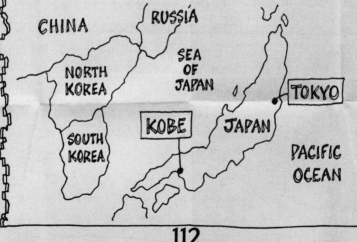

Seismic side effects

Smashing up cities seems shocking enough. But earthquakes have plenty of other nasty surprises in store. Here are some seismic side-effects you might want to steer clear of:

1 Earthquake ups and downs. Earth-shattering earthquakes can change the face of the landscape. So you might have trouble working out where you are. Some land sinks. Some's shoved up several metres into the air. Roads and railway lines that once met in the middle, don't meet anymore. In the 1964 Alaska earthquake, a chunk of land THE SIZE OF FRANCE tilted to one side. It left the fishing village of Cordova so far from the sea that the tide no longer reached the harbour! Leaving the fishermen's boats high and dry. Other normally dry places were flooded.

2 Lethal landslides.

On 31 May 1970, an earthquake with a magnitude of 7.9 shook Peru. But worse was to come. The earthquake triggered off a lethal landslide on Mount Huascaran. It sent millions of tonnes of rock and ice hurtling downhill at devastating speed. The landslide flung boulders and mud into the air and pulverized everything in its path. Including the town of Yungay. Within seconds, the town was smashed to pieces and the townspeople were buried alive. Altogether, on that one dreadful day, about 70,000 people died.

3 Flaming fires. Without doubt, the most sinister side-effects of earthquakes are flaming fires. Often fire does far more damage than the quake itself. Remember the woman cooking ham and eggs in San Francisco? The combination of fire and mostly wooden houses turned breakfast into a nightmare. Another tragic case was the city of Lisbon in Portugal. In November 1755, an awesome earthquake hit the city. With devastating results. Large parts of the city lay in ruins. But worse, much worse, was to come. Within a few hours, sparks from overturned cooking stoves and oil lamps had lit a ferocious fire. For six terrible days, the fire swept through the city before, finally, burning itself out. Before the earthquake, Lisbon had been a beautiful place, filled with palaces, fine houses and priceless works of art. Afterwards, it was burned to a crisp. Luckily (for us), the fire was witnessed first hand by a man called Thomas Chase, an Englishman living in Lisbon. Here's what his letter home might have looked like:

Lisbon, Portugal

November 1755

Dearest Mother,

I hope this letter reaches you safely. The post isn't working too well these days. In fact, nothing's working in Lisbon at present. That wretched earthquake's turned our lives upside down. There's not much of the city left. Anyway, I wanted to let you know I'm safe. I'm one of the lucky ones.

 I was in my bedroom when the ground started shaking. And there was the most dreadful sound I've ever heard. I knew at once that it was an earthquake. It was gentle at first, then it got stronger and stronger. I'm afraid curiosity got the better of me and I ran to the top of the house for a better look. (I know what you're thinking. Stupid boy! And you're right.) I'd nearly made it when the whole house suddenly lurched sideways and knocked me off my feet. Then I felt myself falling. In fact, I'd been thrown out of a window. (Unfortunately, it was on the fourth floor.) I must have passed out because the next thing I remember was my neighbour dragging me out from under a pile of bricks and rubble. He didn't recognize me at first, I looked such a sight.

Anyway, I was pretty shaken up, I can tell you. My poor body was covered in cuts and bruises, and I'd broken my right arm. (I'm afraid that's why my writing's so shaky.) Someone went and fetched my good friend, Mr Forg, and he took me to his house and put me to bed to recover. At last I was safe. Or so I thought. From my bed, I could spy yellow lights flickering outside the window and I could hear the sickening crackle of flames. Would you believe it, the house was on fire! Brave Mr Forg acted quickly. Twice now he's saved my life. At great personal peril, he carried me to safety in the Square, and there I stayed all Saturday night and Sunday. By now, the whole city was on fire. I wept to see it burning out of control.

As I said, dear Mother, despite my wounds, I was lucky. Although I've lost everything, I still have my life. Many of my friends are much worse off. It has been terrible. Terrible.

Anyway, I'll write again soon. And I may see you even sooner. As soon as I'm better, I'm coming home. Until then, please don't worry about me.

Your loving son,
Thomas

excuse thumbprint →

X X X X X

EARTH-SHATTERING FACT FILE

DATE: 1 November 1755
LOCATION: Lisbon, Portugal
TIME: 9.40 a.m.
LENGTH OF SHOCK: about 3 minutes
MAGNITUDE: 8.5–9.0
DEATHS: 60,000
THE SHOCKING FACTS:
- 1 November was All Saints' Day so many people were in church. Many said the earthquake was God's punishment.
- The first tremor was followed by two massive aftershocks.
- Half an hour after the earthquake, three huge waves rolled in from the sea. Thousands of people drowned.

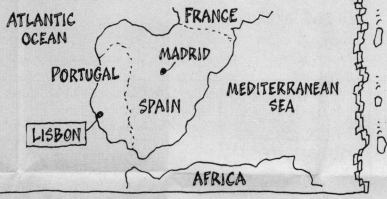

ATLANTIC OCEAN

FRANCE

PORTUGAL

MADRID

SPAIN

MEDITERRANEAN SEA

LISBON

AFRICA

4 Shocking seiches. Spare a thought for the locals who lived around Loch Lochmond in Scotland.

They didn't know there'd been an earthquake in Lisbon. (It took two weeks for Britain to get the news.) So when the loch water suddenly started sloshing violently to and fro, they'd absolutely no idea why. What on Earth was going on? Well, this was another seismic side-effect. Its tricky technical name is a seiche (saysh) wave. And it's caused by all those shock waves shooting through the Earth and shaking up the rocks, including the rocks in loch and lake beds.

5 Terrible tsunamis (soo-naa-mees). A tsunami (that's Japanese for 'harbour wave') is a gigantic wave triggered off by an earthquake under the sea. Some people call them tidal waves, but they're nothing to do with tides at all. Tsunamis don't look much to start with. In fact, they can pass ships by without being seen. But once they reach land, it's a different story. Are you brave enough to find out how a tsunami grows? What happens is this:

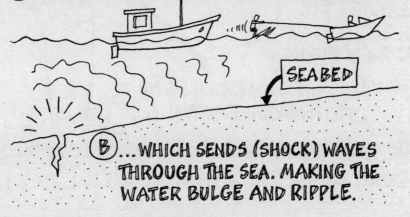

Ⓐ AN EARTHQUAKE SHAKES THE SEABED...

SEABED

Ⓑ ...WHICH SENDS (SHOCK) WAVES THROUGH THE SEA. MAKING THE WATER BULGE AND RIPPLE.

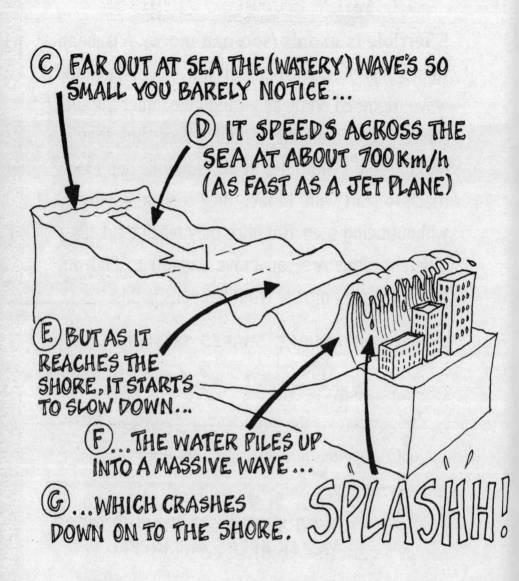

Ⓒ FAR OUT AT SEA THE (WATERY) WAVE'S SO SMALL YOU BARELY NOTICE...

Ⓓ IT SPEEDS ACROSS THE SEA AT ABOUT 700 km/h (AS FAST AS A JET PLANE)

Ⓔ BUT AS IT REACHES THE SHORE, IT STARTS TO SLOW DOWN...

Ⓕ ...THE WATER PILES UP INTO A MASSIVE WAVE...

Ⓖ ...WHICH CRASHES DOWN ON TO THE SHORE. SPLASHH!

Horrible Health Warning

Tsunamis are horribly dangerous. As they smash on to the shore, they wash everything away. Buildings, boats, people and even WHOLE VILLAGES. Tsunamis can be five times as tall as your house. That's an awful lot of water. Trouble is you don't notice them until it's too late. So if the sea looks as if it's been sucked away from the shore, GET OUT OF THE WAY. FAST! Chances are a tsunami's around the corner, ready to rear its ugly head.

Terror in the Indian Ocean

On 26 December 2004, a truly terrifying tsunami struck coasts right around the Indian Ocean... WITHOUT ANY WARNING. By the time the wall of water had drained away, hundreds of thousands of people had been left dead, injured or homeless. It was one of the worst natural disasters the world has ever seen.

The tsunami was triggered by a colossal underwater quake off the coast of Indonesia, and raced across the Indian Ocean faster than a jet plane. Thirty minutes later, it smashed into the island of Sumatra, rearing up to the height of a three-storey building. Leaving Sumatra, the tsumami continued its trail of destruction and headed for southern Thailand. Tourists and locals alike were hit by thousands of tonnes of water, crashing down on them. Many were drowned in their homes or hotel rooms. Others were dragged out to sea. Next in the tsunami's path was Sri Lanka, smashing the shoreline to smithereens and wiping out whole towns and villages. After that, it crashed in the Maldives, then the east coast of Africa…

In the days after the tsunami, the appalling scale of the tragedy began to unfold. Whole communities had been wiped off the map, and the death toll was rising all the time. Many people had lost everything — homes, belongings, livelihoods…and loved ones. Immediately, the countries affected were declared disaster zones and help began pouring in from the stunned outside world. But the tsunami's traumatised victims had lived for a nightmare, and, many years later, they are still trying to rebuild their shattered lives.

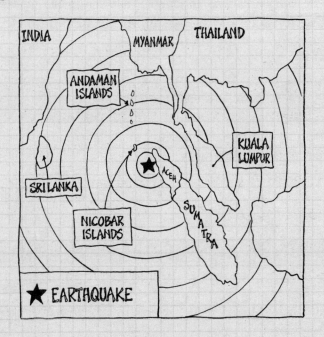

EARTH-SHATTERING FACT FILE

DATE: 26 December 2004
LOCATION: Off the west coast of Northern Sumatra
TIME: 7.59 a.m.
LENGTH OF SHOCK: about ten minutes
MAGNITUDE: 9.1
DEATHS: 230,000
THE SHOCKING FACTS:

• An estimated five million people were affected by the tsunami. More than 230,000 were killed; 500,000 were injured and 1.7 million were left homeless.

• Fourteen countries were hit by the waves. The worst hit was Indonesia, especially Sumatra. The northern city of Bandeh Aceh was reduced to rubble in just 15 minutes.

• In Bandeh Aceh, a 2,600-tonne ship, the Apung 1, was flung more than 2 kilometres inland by the tsunami's terrifying force.

• Elephants in Thailand seem to sense the wave coming and began behaving oddly, stamping their feet and running away.

Horrible (tsunami) Health Warning

After this devastating disaster, a tsunami warning system was set up in the Indian Ocean. Put simple, it works like this. Pressure sensors on the sea bed detect a tsunami and send alerts to a series of ground centres. Warnings can then be flashed out, although they are still not getting to enough people, quickly enough.

In future, the numbers of people living on shaky ground is likely to go up and up. After all, quake zones cover large parts of the Earth and you can't avoid them all. Besides, shaking aside, they're often pretty pleasant places to live. So what can be done to make life safer? Time to call the earth-shattering experts in. . .

EARTH-SHATTERING EXPERT!

EARTHQUAKE EXPERTS

Scientists who study earth-shattering earthquakes are called seismologists (size-moll-ow-gists). And no, their name's got nothing to do with the size of their brains. Though they'd probably like you to think so. Forget pictures of batty professors in long, white coats snoozing away in dusty laboratories. Seismologists are scientists under pressure. Their tricky task is to work out what makes awesome earthquakes tick. But it isn't as simple as it sounds. Earthquakes are horribly unpredictable. No one knows where and when the next quake will hit. Does this put the stressed-out seismologists off? No way. It just makes them keener than ever to crack on and break new ground.

Could you be a seismologist?

Do you have what it takes to be a seismologist? Would you be able to stand the strain? Try this quick quiz to find out. Better still, try it out on your geography teacher.

1 Are you a whizz at maths? Yes/No

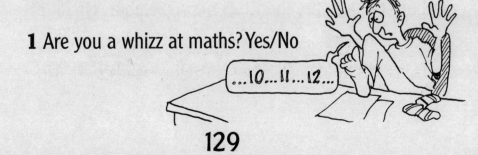

2 Fabulous at physics? Yes/No

3 Marvellous at map-reading? Yes/No

4 Have you got a good imagination? Yes/No

5 Have you got eyes in the back of your head? Yes/No

6 Do you fancy travelling to exotic locations? Yes/No

ANSWER

1 You'll need to be. A lot of seismology means collecting scientific information and feeding it into computers. Then working out what on Earth

it all means. How do you do this? By doing horribly long and complicated sums, that's how. So you need to be pretty nifty with numbers.

2 Physics is useful for finding out how shock waves travel through the Earth. Unfortunately, shock waves don't go in nice, straight lines. That would be too easy. So plotting their path from A (the earthquake's focus deep underground) to B (the epicentre on the surface of the ground) isn't straightforward either. As they pass through different types of soil or rock, the wayward waves get reflected back on themselves or bent at an angle (technically speaking, bending's called refraction). Either way, it sends them speeding off in all directions. And guess what? Yep, reflection and refraction are bits of physics.

3 If you get lost finding your way to school

(especially if it's geography test day), a map won't help you much. But if you're really serious about seismology, map-reading's a must. I mean, how else will you find the fault?

4 No, I don't mean imagining things like your teacher telling you you're a genius. That really would be a dream come true. This is the sort of imagination that lets you think up a 3-D picture of what's inside the Earth. Without actually being able to see it. It's essential because this is where earthquakes actually happen. But it's tricky because there aren't any maps. It's a bit

like you trying to find that bag of crisps you know you hid under your bed, IN THE DARK.

5 Of course, you don't really need eyes in the back of your head. (Think of the fortune you'd have to spend in cool sunshades!) But you do need to be observant.

So are you on the ball or would you sleep through anything? Try filling in this real-life earthquake questionnaire. It's for finding out how you'd react in an earthquake. Even if you've never lived through a real-life earthquake, think about how you might answer the questions if you had.

EARTHQUAKE QUESTIONNAIRE

① Where were you when the earthquake happened?
② What time was the tremor?
③ Did you feel any vibrations?
④ What did you hear?
⑤ Were you indoors or out?
⑥ Were you sitting/standing/lying down/active/sleeping/listening to the radio/watching TV?
⑦ Were you frightened?
⑧ Did any doors or windows rattle?
⑨ Did anything else rattle?
⑩ Did any hanging objects swing?
⑪ Did anything fall?
⑫ Was there any damage?

6 You'll have the chance to visit seismic stations all around the world in such unusual places as the Arctic, the Antarctic, the Himalayas, Africa and New Zealand. Better get your atlas out!

How do you think you'd do?

Snapshots of the stars

Don't worry if seismology's got you stumped. Sit back and let the real earthquake experts take the strain. Are you ready to rub shoulders with some of the most shockingly clever scientists ever? Here's Sid to introduce you to five real brainboxes...

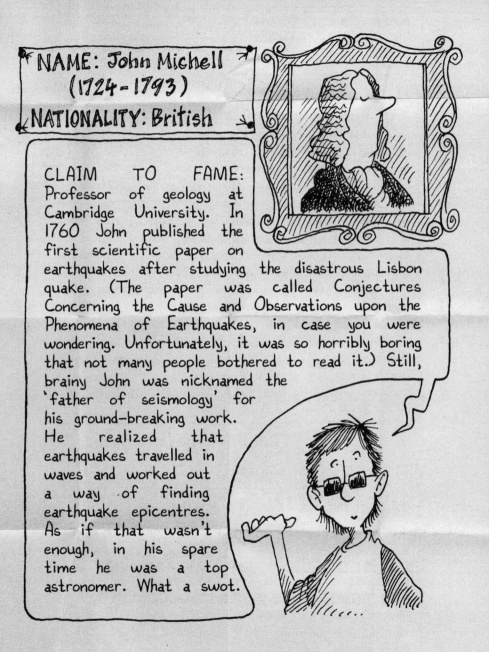

NAME: John Michell
(1724 - 1793)
NATIONALITY: British

CLAIM TO FAME: Professor of geology at Cambridge University. In 1760 John published the first scientific paper on earthquakes after studying the disastrous Lisbon quake. (The paper was called Conjectures Concerning the Cause and Observations upon the Phenomena of Earthquakes, in case you were wondering. Unfortunately, it was so horribly boring that not many people bothered to read it.) Still, brainy John was nicknamed the 'father of seismology' for his ground-breaking work. He realized that earthquakes travelled in waves and worked out a way of finding earthquake epicentres. As if that wasn't enough, in his spare time he was a top astronomer. What a swot.

137

NAME: Robert Mallet
(1810 – 1881)
NATIONALITY: Irish

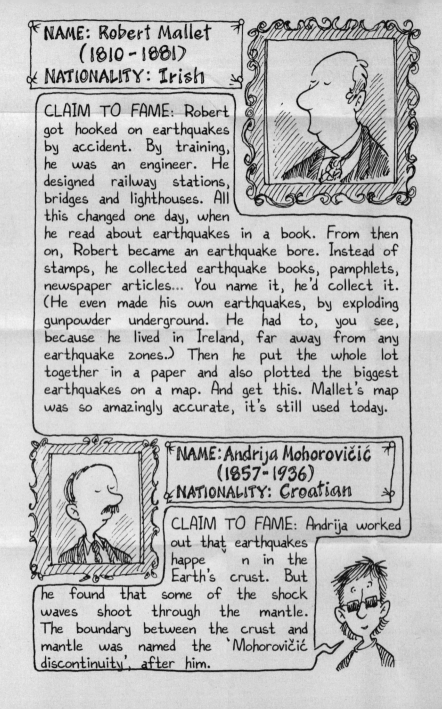

CLAIM TO FAME: Robert got hooked on earthquakes by accident. By training, he was an engineer. He designed railway stations, bridges and lighthouses. All this changed one day, when he read about earthquakes in a book. From then on, Robert became an earthquake bore. Instead of stamps, he collected earthquake books, pamphlets, newspaper articles... You name it, he'd collect it. (He even made his own earthquakes, by exploding gunpowder underground. He had to, you see, because he lived in Ireland, far away from any earthquake zones.) Then he put the whole lot together in a paper and also plotted the biggest earthquakes on a map. And get this. Mallet's map was so amazingly accurate, it's still used today.

NAME: Andrija Mohorovičić
(1857 – 1936)
NATIONALITY: Croatian

CLAIM TO FAME: Andrija worked out that earthquakes happen in the Earth's crust. But he found that some of the shock waves shoot through the mantle. The boundary between the crust and mantle was named the 'Mohorovičić discontinuity', after him.

Thankfully, it was such a mouthful, it's now been shortened to Moho. Anyway, Moho was a real clever clogs. Not only was he brilliant at physics and maths, geology and meteorology, he also spoke fluent Croatian, English, French, Italian, Latin, Ancient Greek and Czech. So he could say "earthquake" in seven different languages!

NAME: Beno Gutenberg
(1889-1960)
NATIONALITY: American

CLAIM TO FAME: Gutenberg spent years studying seismic waves and working out how they travelled. He also helped Charles Richter work out the, er, Richter scale. (So strictly speaking that should have been the Gutenberg-Richter scale.) Again with his pal Richter, Beno showed that three-quarters of earthquakes happen around the shaky Pacific Ocean. But you knew that already. Brainy Beno's best-known books included *Earthquakes in North America* and *The Seismicity of the Earth*. OK, I know they sound too boring to read.

NAME: John Milne (1850-1913)
NATIONALITY: British

CLAIM TO FAME: Brilliant John Milne really shook things up by inventing the first practical seismograph (size-mow-graf). That's a posh bit of equipment for measuring earthquakes. Here's the amazing true story of his shocking discovery...

A shocking discovery

John Milne was born in Liverpool, England. He trained at the Royal School of Mines in London and became a mining engineer. (That's someone in charge of building mines underground. Sounds boring – gettit? – but someone had to do it.) When John was just 25 years old, he was offered the job of a lifetime. He became professor of geology and mining at the Imperial College of Engineering in Tokyo, Japan. Posh, or what?

There was just one teeny little snag. . . Japan was a very long way from Liverpool and John hated the sea. (Which was strange for someone who loved to travel. As a young man he was always on the move.) Instead he went most of the way overland, through Europe and Russia. It took 11 long, tiring months to reach Japan. And to make matters worse, on John's very first night in his new home, Tokyo was struck by a (small-ish)

earthquake! What a shock! And it wouldn't be John's last. As you know, Japan stands on horribly shaky ground. John later wrote that there were earthquakes "for breakfast, dinner, supper and to sleep on". But for the time being, he had other things on his mind. His new job kept him on his toes. Especially the bit where he had to climb to the tops of active volcanoes to inspect their fiery craters. Luckily, the volcanoes didn't blow their tops else daring John would have been a goner. Then who knows what seismologists would have done.

In 1880 a powerful earthquake shook the nearby city of Yokohama. It was enough to make John turn his back on volcanoes and concentrate on earthquakes instead. Immediately, he called a meeting of like-minded scientists and set up the Seismological Society of Japan. (When John put his mind to something, he didn't waste any time you see.) From then on, there was no stopping him. Studying earthquakes became his life's work. But first he needed to find out more about them. The question was how? Then clever John had a brainwave. He needed information and he needed it fast. (And people didn't have telephones or the internet then.) So he sent every post office for miles around a bundle of stamped, self-addressed postcards. All the postmaster (or mistress) had to do was fill in one card every week and post it back to John, describing any tremors. They didn't even need to buy a stamp. Pretty cunning, eh? What's more, it worked! Soon John was swamped with mail bags. There were postcards everywhere. From the answers he got, he was able to draw up detailed maps of every single shock and shudder to shake Japan.

But John still wasn't satisfied. Eyewitness accounts were all very well but you couldn't really rely on them. People were always exaggerating or playing things down. For example, you might accidentally tick the answer 'huge' to describe the size of a tremor, when all along you meant 'quite small' but you didn't want your postcard to look dead boring. Anyway, what John desperately needed was a posh machine for measuring earthquakes accurately. Various ingenious instruments had been invented but none of them worked very well. Did John give up? Did he, heck. No, he went and invented the first modern seismograph (size-moh-graf). It recorded the shock waves from an earthquake so scientists could study and measure them. When an earthquake struck and shook the seismograph, a pin or pen traced the pattern of shaking on to a piece of smoked paper or glass. It was brilliant. Earth-shatteringly brilliant.

Getting the shakes

Basic seismographs haven't changed much since John Milne's time. Which just shows how bloomin' brainy he was. But how on Earth do these marvellous machines work? Do you need to be a genius geographer to use one? Or is it something even your teacher could grasp? Who better to guide you through the muddle than Sid's very own Uncle Stan, the handyman.

MORNIN', STAN HERE. NOW WHAT'S THIS ABOUT SEISMOGRAPHS? PESKY THINGS, I AGREE. NEVER MIND, YOU STICK WITH ME AND WE'LL SOON HAVE THE BEAUTY UP AND RUNNING. FIRST YOU NEED TO GET TO KNOW HOW ALL THE BITS AND PIECES WORK.

Your Seismograph...

frame (fixed to the ground)

spring

heavy weight

squiggly pattern

shaking Earth

rotating roll of paper

scratchy pen

STAN'S TOP TIP: Don't worry if your seismograph doesn't look exactly like this one. There are lots of different types. Some use a beam of light to trace the pattern on to photographic film. Others record the wave pattern electronically or digitally. (The last ones are probably best left to the experts, in my view.)

HOW IT WORKS...

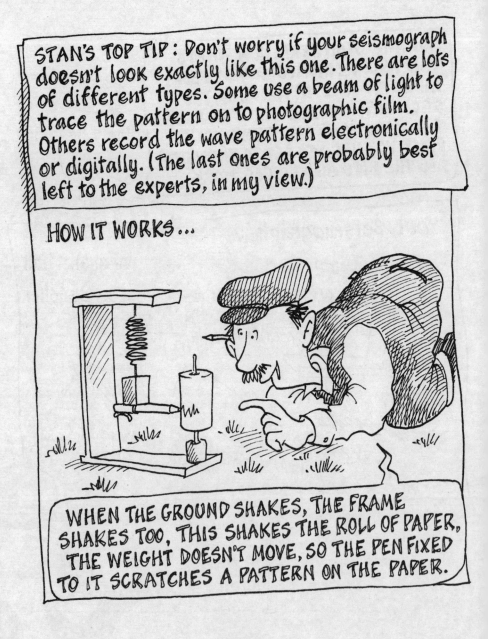

WHEN THE GROUND SHAKES, THE FRAME SHAKES TOO. THIS SHAKES THE ROLL OF PAPER, THE WEIGHT DOESN'T MOVE, SO THE PEN FIXED TO IT SCRATCHES A PATTERN ON THE PAPER.

Checking the print-out

The posh technical term for the squiggly lines on the paper is a seismogram (size-mow-gram). Oh they like making things difficult, these scientists. The squiggles show the shock waves from an earthquake. The bigger the squiggles, the bigger the quake. Still with me? Good. Now you've just got to decipher your seismogram, and you're home and dry.

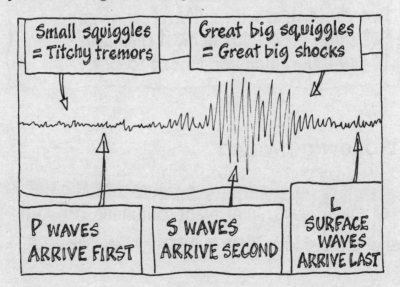

Small squiggles = Titchy tremors

Great big squiggles = Great big shocks

P WAVES ARRIVE FIRST

S WAVES ARRIVE SECOND

L SURFACE WAVES ARRIVE LAST

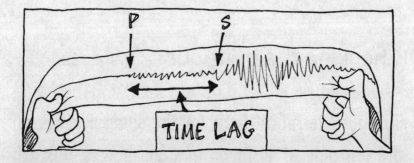

The size of the waves is used to work out the earthquake's magnitude. The closer the earthquake, the bigger the waves.

STAN'S TOP TIP: For more accurate readings, try burying your seismograph underground. I've done that with quite a few of mine. But don't forget to check it regularly. If you can remember where to dig...

Worldwide watch

For many years, John Milne continued his earth-shattering studies. Then in 1895 disaster struck. Fire broke out and destroyed John's home and his precious observatory. Luckily, John and his wife escaped unhurt but his priceless collection of books and instruments went up in smoke. Years of hard work were lost in minutes. Shattered, John left Japan and returned to England, but he didn't stop his earthquake watch. In his new home, on the Isle of Wight, he built himself a brand-new observatory, complete with a brand-new seismograph. It was the first of many. By 1902, he'd set up similar observatories all over the world to keep a 24-hour eye on earthquakes.

I'LL BE GLAD WHEN THE NEW EQUIPMENT GETS HERE!

OH, STOP COMPLAINING!

Today, the Global Seismographic Network has monitoring stations all over the world, measuring earthquakes as they happen. Using the latest high-tech seismographs, they can map the entire location and shape of a fault in just a matter of hours. And sound the alarm. . .

The first ever seismograph was invented in China in about 130 CE. It was built by Zhang Heng, a brilliant mathematician, astronomer, map-maker, painter, poet, and, er, seismograph-maker. (Don't some people make you sick?) But it didn't look like any seismograph you'd see today. It was a big bronze vase ringed with bronze dragons and toads. Each dragon held a bronze ball in its mouth. Inside the vase hung a heavy pendulum. When the Earth shook, the pendulum tilted, making the dragon furthest from the earthquake's epicentre drop its ball. Did this convoluted contraption work? Incredibly, it did!

MAY I HAVE MY BALL BACK, PLEASE?

TEACHER TEASER

If you're thinking of taking up seismology seriously, you'll need more than a seismograph. Why not baffle your teacher with the names of some other impressive-sounding instruments. Try this one for starters:

PLEASE, MISS, MY CREEPMETER'S ON THE BLINK!

GO AND SEE THE SCHOOL NURSE

What on Earth are you talking about?

ANSWER

A creepmeter's a useful instrument for measuring how much the ground moves in a fault between earthquakes. (And has nothing to do with being a creepy swot and giving your teacher apples.)

If your creepmeter's really on the blink, you could be in for a bumpy ride. To be a real earthquake expert, you might need a strainmeter and a tiltmeter too. A strainmeter measures how much the rocks are squeezed or stretched. A tiltmeter works out how much the ground, er, tilts. Oh, so you knew that already!

If you're itching to get out and get on with your measuring (are you raving mad?), don't go just yet. Your seismograph might be up and running but it can only get the measure of an earthquake AFTER THE EARTHQUAKE'S OVER. It can't tell you where a quake might happen next. So before you go charging off, read the next chapter. Please. It might be a matter of life and death.

SHOCKING WARNING SIGNS

Never mind fancy instruments with fine-sounding names. What if your new-fangled seismograph breaks down under the strain? Then you'd be in serious trouble. Besides, earth-shattering earthquakes are so horribly hard to predict, seismologists need all the extra help they can get. So how on Earth can you tell if and when an earthquake's about to strike? Is it even possible? Could you spot the shocking warning signs?

OOOOOOH! EARTHQUAKE

Could you be a seismologist?

The ground starts shaking and you're scared stiff. You run into the street, just before your house collapses behind you. You've lost everything, your best trainers, your precious smartphone and your tablet. But you're lucky to be alive. If only you'd known to expect an earthquake. Then you could have grabbed  your belongings and got out of there, fast. Are there any warning signs you could have looked out for? Take a look at the clues below. Seismologists think they may be tell-tale signs of stress. Tick the box if you see them.

1 Weird water. Weird things happen to water just before earthquakes. For months or even years before, water levels in wells get lower and lower. Then, suddenly, the water shoots back up again. Other watery signs include foaming lakes, boiling seas and fountains that won't stop flowing. See if you notice anything strange next time you have

TICK IF YOU'VE SPOTTED

a bath. (Remember the bath? It's that big tub thing in the bathroom?)

2 Gushing geysers.
Geysers are gigantic jets of steam and scalding water that's heated to boiling point by hot rocks underground. Then it bursts into the air. You could set your watch by certain geysers. Take Old Faithful in California, USA. It usually erupts roughly

every hour. Regular as clockwork. Except before an earthquake, that is. Then it becomes more unpredictable. Scientists aren't sure why this happens but they're not taking any chances. They've got a webcam watching this gushing geyser 24 hours a day.

3 Ghastly gases. Radon is a ghastly gas given off by underground rocks. It seeps to the surface in springs and stream water. Before an earthquake, scientists have noticed that the seeping starts to speed up. It seems that stressed-out rocks release

more radon. This is exactly what happened just before the 1995 Kobe quake. Unfortunately, the warning signs were ignored.

4 Frightful foreshocks.

Before a big quake you often get lots of little mini-quakes. Seismologists call them foreshocks. They get bigger and stronger as the stress builds up. And they're pretty good clues, if they happen. Trouble is you sometimes don't feel

any foreshocks at all. Not even the tiniest tremble. Or if you do, they may just fizzle out again, without doing any damage.

5 Bright lights. If the sky fills with fireworks (and it's not 5 November yet), watch out. An earthquake might be around the corner. An hour before the Kobe quake, people saw flashes of red, green and blue light streaking across the sky. The tricky technical name

WOW! PRETTY

TICK IF YOU'VE SPOTTED

for this is fractoluminescence (frakto-loom-in-essence) which means broken lights. Scientists think the lights are caused by smashed-up bits of sparkly quartz, a crusty crystal found in rocks.

6 Stormy weather. For years, people believed in 'earthquake weather'. Trouble is, they couldn't agree what it was. Some said it was calm weather with clear, blue skies. Others said it was stormy weather with frightening lightning and pouring rain. Who was

TICK IF YOU'VE SPOTTED

right? Neither, I'm afraid. You can blame the weather for lots of things, like not being able to go out on your bike. But you can't blame it for earthquakes.

How many warning signs did you spot? Hopefully, you won't have ticked anything. Which means you're perfectly safe and sound, and don't need to worry.

163

In October 1989, a seismologist in California detected electrical signals coming from the ground. The signals got stronger and stronger. Then, 12 days later, the earth-shattering Loma Prieta earthquake struck. Were the signals sounding a warning? The shocked scientist certainly thought so. He reckoned the stressed-out rocks had set the signals off. (Note: before you get too excited, guess what? Yep. Other horrible seismologists totally disagree!)

Alarming animals

If you don't think any of these warnings would work, don't worry. Try some old-fashioned folklore instead. Some people say animals start acting oddly before earthquakes. Scientists think animals may be reacting to very high-pitched sounds that we can't hear, coming from tiny cracks around the area that's about to quake. So watch out if your pet cat stops chasing mice or your pet dog starts purring. You may be in for a nasty shock. Which of the following wildlife warning signs are too way-out to be true?

a) Catfish wriggle and leap out of water. TRUE/ FALSE?

MEEOOWW!

b) Rats panic and run away. TRUE/FALSE

c) Pet dogs and cats go
missing. TRUE/FALSE?

d) Wild animals like tigers behave like, er, pussycats.
TRUE/FALSE?

e) Honey bees abandon
their hives? TRUE/FALSE?

f) Worms worm their way to the
surface? TRUE/FALSE?

OOOH! DAYLIGHT

g) Crocodiles lose their cool. TRUE/FALSE?

h) Goldfish go mad and jump out of their bowls. TRUE/FALSE?

ANSWER

Incredibly, they're all TRUE. But what on Earth sends these animals into such a spin? Well, it might be because they can hear very low rumbling sounds coming from the Earth. Too low for human ears to hear. Or they might sense changes in the Earth's magnetic field (the Earth's insides act like a very weak magnet). One thing's for certain. Woe betide those spoilsport scientists who tell you it's all a load of nonsense. They'd better not mess with a cross crocodile. Or they might end up as its lunch!

CHOMP!
CHOMP!

Cracking clues or pure coincidence?

So do any of these warning signs really work? Are they crucial quake-busting clues? Or just amazing coincidences? To tell you the truth, there's no easy answer. Sometimes they work. And sometimes they don't work. In the shaky world of seismology, you can't rely on anything. As you're about to find out when you read these two shocking true stories. . .

Lucky escape

On 4 February 1975 an earth-shattering earthquake struck the city of Haicheng in China. But instead of an estimated 150,000 deaths (1 million people lived in the city), only around 2,000 people lost their lives. It could have been worse. Much worse. But for several months before the quake hit, people started noticing weird warnings signs. Hibernating snakes woke up suddenly and slithered sleepily out of their holes, even though it was still winter and they weren't meant to wake up until the spring. Groups of rats were seen running round in circles. What's more,  there were 500 foreshocks in the space of four days. It all added up to a massive shock. Fortunately, the authorities decided to take notice of these warning signs. They couldn't predict exactly when an earthquake might strike, but they weren't prepared to take any chances. Finally, on 3 February, the city was evacuated. People got ready to spend the freezing night outdoors in tents and straw shelters. At 7.36 p.m., the earthquake struck. . .

It was a big one, with a magnitude of 7.0 – the evacuation had come in the nick of time.

Total disaster

But had the warnings signs done the trick? Could they really be relied on? Many seismologists dismissed the prediction as a fluke. True, thousands of lives had been saved. But it could have been a lucky guess. Were they right? Eighteen months later, at 3.42 a.m. on 28 July 1976, another Chinese city was struck by another awesome earthquake. This quake had a magnitude of 7.5. But the people of Tangshan weren't so lucky. There were no warning signs whatsoever. No startled snakes. No rattled rats. No rumbling foreshocks. Nothing. In little over a minute, more than 655,000 people were killed. Almost 800,000 more were injured. The city itself was completely demolished. It was one of the most devastating earthquakes ever. And nobody saw it coming…

Can we really predict earthquakes?

Will earthquakes ever be properly predicted? Can seismologists ever hope to stay one step ahead? Horribly simple questions, you might think. Horribly simple questions ... with impossibly tricky answers. So tricky that even the earth-shattering experts can't agree. Just listen to these two, for starters. . .

No! It's not like forecasting the weather, you know. We can't give nice, precise predictions. I mean, we can't say an earthquake of a certain size will strike a certain place at a certain time. It's not like saying it'll rain in Spain next Tuesday. (Not that weather forecasts are always right.) It simply isn't possible. We just don't know enough about the Earth's insides. Besides, some earthquakes strike without any warning. So there's no way of telling they're even on their way.

Yes! We can give very general warnings. We can say a place can expect a big earthquake sometime this century. But we can't say exactly when or where. It's all down to probability. A bit like you saying you might get round to doing your homework sometime this week. Not horribly exact, is it? But we can pinpoint possible danger zones on a map. So people have time to prepare. OK, it's not much. But it's better than nothing.

If seismologists could even give 20 seconds' (yes, seconds) warning, they could save thousands of lives. But scientists have to be careful. A false alarm could be fatal. If they order an evacuation, and no earthquake hits, people might not be so keen to listen next time. Even if they could predict an earthquake, of course, they couldn't do anything to stop it happening. And that's the only thing they know for certain!

SURVIVING THE SHOCK

OK, so your pet cat's left home. DON'T PANIC. Your cat's most likely off chasing mice. It's very, very unlikely that this means an earthquake's about to strike. But you never know. So what would you do if you found yourself on horribly shaky ground? How would you cope? No idea? Luckily Sid's here with his earth-shattering guide to earthquake survival. Don't go to bed without it...

175

Earth-shattering earthquake survival guide

Hi, Sid here. If you live in a quake zone, it pays to be prepared. Better safe than sorry, I always say. Places used to earth-shattering earthquakes practise regular earthquake drills. They're a bit like the fire drills you have at school, except you don't have to spend hours standing in the playground in the soaking rain. Thank goodness. Anyway, to practise staying safe in an earthquake, here are some essential dos and don'ts:

DO...

• **Stock up on supplies.** Pack an emergency survival kit. You'll need a fire extinguisher, a torch (with spare batteries), a first-aid kit, tinned food (don't forget a tin-opener and food for your cat –

he's bound to come home in the end), bottled water (enough for three days), sleeping bags or blankets, warm clothes and sturdy shoes (for walking over rubble and broken glass). Keep these things somewhere handy and make sure everyone in your family or class knows where they are.

• **Listen to the radio.** Keep a radio (and more spare batteries) in your emergency kit. After the quake, communications may be cut for several days or even weeks. So stay in touch by tuning in to your radio for information and advice.

- **Be prepared.** Make sure everyone in your family or class knows what to do. (Practise beforehand.) Fix up a meeting place for after the quake in case you get split up.

- **Turn off the gas and electricity.** The quake may break gas pipes and snap power lines. So you'll need your torch for seeing in the dark. Never, ever light a match. If there's been a gas leak, everything could go up in flames.

• **Crouch under a sturdy table.** Or under your desk if you're at school. Cover your head with a cushion or pillow, and press your face into your arm. This'll protect your head and eyes from broken glass and flying objects. Hold on tight to the table leg. Now don't move until the shaking stops. Remember, DUCK, COVER AND HOLD ON. (By the way, never stand in a doorway. Doorframes are not horribly strong.)

DON'T...

• **Rush outside.** Wait until the house stops shaking before you rush outside. Otherwise you might get hit by flying glass or debris. (Or you might fall out of a window. Remember poor Thomas Chase?) The general rule is: if you're inside, stay inside and if you're outside, stay put.

• **Use the stairs.** If you live in a block of flats, or you're at school, stay away from the stairs. At least until the shaking's stopped. You could easily fall or get crushed. Whatever happens, don't use the lift. If the power's cut, you'll be trapped.

I THINK WE'RE GOING TO BE HERE FOR A WHILE

OH, GOODIE!

• **Stand by a building.** Once the shaking's stopped and you can go outside, find an open space to stand in. Stay away from buildings, trees, chimneys, power lines, and anything that might fall on top of you.

• **Go for a drive.** At least, not until the shaking's over. If you're in a car, slow down and stop in an open space. But watch out for falling rocks and landslides. And don't go anywhere near a bridge. It'll probably collapse with you on top. Stay inside the car until the shaking's stopped.

• **Use the phone.** For the first few days after the earthquake, don't use the phone. If it's really, really urgent, OK. But don't phone your friends for a chat. It might clog up the phone lines and stop emergency calls getting through.

Earthquake rescue

Phew! You've made it. But you've been lucky. In the chaos that follows a major earthquake, thousands of people may be injured or killed. Many are buried under collapsed buildings. Leaving the rescue teams with no time to lose. But it's a horribly risky job. At any moment, a building could come crashing down on top of the rescuers, especially if small aftershocks hit it. Besides, they may only have tools like pickaxes, spades, or even their bare hands to work with. Even with the latest high-tech kit, like heartbeat and breathing detectors and even search-and-rescue robots, it's a race against time. (Specially trained dogs are also used. Not so high-tech but brilliant at sniffing out survivors.) The rescuers know they have to work fast. Without much air or water, trapped victims may only have days to live. For some people, help arrives too late if it arrives at all. But it isn't all bad news. Sometimes, somehow, against all the odds, miracles do happen. Take the extraordinary events in Mexico City. . .

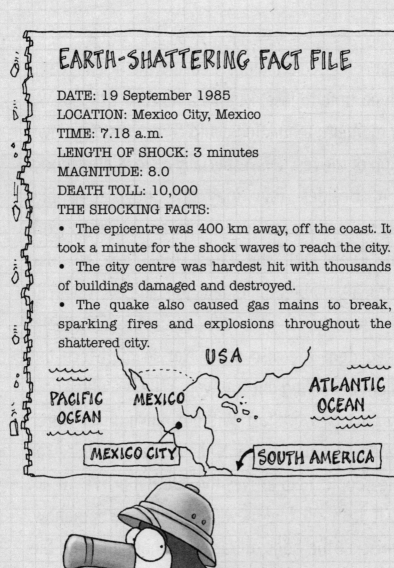

EARTH-SHATTERING FACT FILE

DATE: 19 September 1985
LOCATION: Mexico City, Mexico
TIME: 7.18 a.m.
LENGTH OF SHOCK: 3 minutes
MAGNITUDE: 8.0
DEATH TOLL: 10,000
THE SHOCKING FACTS:

- The epicentre was 400 km away, off the coast. It took a minute for the shock waves to reach the city.
- The city centre was hardest hit with thousands of buildings damaged and destroyed.
- The quake also caused gas mains to break, sparking fires and explosions throughout the shattered city.

USA

PACIFIC OCEAN

MEXICO

ATLANTIC OCEAN

MEXICO CITY

SOUTH AMERICA

The Daily Globe 🌐

29 September 1985, Mexico City

MIRACLE BABIES IN RESCUE SHOCK

Ten days after a massive earthquake devastated the city, rescuers are celebrating a miracle. Two new-born babies have been pulled alive from the ruins of the maternity hospital. A doctor who examined the babies told our reporter, "It's wonderful news. Babies are pretty tough, you know. When they suffer a really big shock, they're able to slow their bodies right down. It's like animals hibernating. That way, they can stay alive for a surprisingly long time without food or water."

The babies had a very lucky escape. The multi-storey hospital in which they were born collapsed like a house of cards. Its twisted remains are all that are left. About a thousand doctors, nurses and patients were buried under the rubble.

TOTAL COLLAPSE

PET RESCUE

OH, BABY!

It's the same story all over the city. Since the quake struck, exhausted rescuers have worked around the clock to pull survivors out. As the days wear on, their task becomes even grimmer. Now there are mainly dead bodies to bring out. But finding the babies has given the rescuers a much-needed boost. One man told us, with tears in his eyes, "It's like a beacon of hope in all the misery and blackness. We'd almost given up hope of finding anyone else alive. These little ones have given us the strength we needed to carry on with our efforts."

Earth-shattering fact

When an earth-shattering 7.2 earthquake struck Turkey in October 2011, five people had a very close shave. Trapped in the ruins of a collapsed building, they managed to call the rescue team . . . on their mobile phone! They were later pulled out, battered and bruised, but lucky to be alive.

Quake-proof construction

In an earth-shattering earthquake, it's not shock that kills people but collapsing buildings. So what can be done to cut the risk? Well, architects and engineers are already working on the problem. They're trying to build quake-proof buildings that can really stand the strain.

BUILDERS FOR HIRE

HOUSE STARTING TO SWAY?

WALLS STARTING TO CRACK?

NEED QUAKE-PROOFING YOU CAN RELY ON?

LOOK NO FURTHER...

SACKED

RUMBLE, CRUMBLE, TUMBLE & SONS
BUILDERS
LET US TAKE THE STRAIN

SMALL PRINT: DON'T BLAME US IF YOUR HOUSE FALLS DOWN. WITH EARTHQUAKES THERE ARE NO GUARANTEES. QUAKE-PROOFING MIGHT DO THE TRICK. THEN AGAIN, IT MIGHT NOT. SORRY.

Want to make sure your house survives the shock and stays standing? But daren't trust the small ads? Why not do it yourself? Sneak a look in this dusty but helpful DIY manual to find out what you need to do. And if you can't tell one end of a hammer from the other, don't worry. Here's Sid's Uncle Stan back to help you with more of his handy hints and tips.

BUILDING FOR BEGINNERS

Lesson 1: Why do buildings fall down?

Before you learn how to keep your house standing up, you need to find out why it might fall down. Are you brave enough to shake your house down?

WHAT YOU NEED:

- A SMALL PLASTIC BOTTLE OF ORANGE SQUASH* (FOR THE HOUSE)

- A PIECE OF CARD (FOR THE EARTH)

WHAT TO DO:

① PLACE THE BOTTLE ON THE CARD

② PUSH THE CARD SLOWLY BACKWARDS AND FORWARDS

③ DO THIS AGAIN REALLY QUICKLY THIS TIME

④ DO THIS AGAIN AT A SPEED SOMEWHERE BETWEEN THE TWO

What happens?

a) The bottle shakes a bit but doesn't fall over.

b) The bottle sways but doesn't fall over.

c) The bottle sways a lot and falls over.

Answer: It depends how fast you push the card. If you push slowly, the bottle wobbles a bit but doesn't fall over. If you push quickly, it sways at the top but still stays up. But if you push at a speed somewhere between the two, the bottle falls over. This is because it's shaking at exactly the same frequency** as the card. It's the same when an earthquake strikes. If a building shakes at exactly the same frequency as the ground, it soon topples over.

* You can drink the squash when you've finished this chapter. DIY can be thirsty work. Don't use fizzy pop though. It'll spurt all over the place when you open the bottle and make a terrible mess.

** Frequency's the tricky technical term for the number of shock waves passing through it each second.

191

STAN'S HANDY HINTS NO.1

Pick the shape carefully when you're planning your house. Take a look at these two barmy buildings. Which one do you think would work best in an earthquake?

Give up? In fact, they both work brilliantly. The pyramid shape, on the left, is great in an earthquake. This particular building's in San Francisco. In the 1989 Loma Prieta quake, its 49 storeys swayed a bit but didn't fall down. The beehive shape, on the right, is another cracking design. It's short and squat and keeps its feet firmly on the ground.

LESSON 2: STOPPING THE SHAKING

OK, so now you know why buildings fall down in an earthquake. But how can you keep them standing? The first thing you've got to do is cut down the shaking. If your house doesn't shake so much, it's less likely to tumble. There's a range of techniques you can use. All tried and tested by yours truly. You could. . .

• **Fit shock absorbers.** Shock absorbers are giant rubber pads used to soak up shock waves. Build them into a wall and you'll cut down the shaking. They've been used on loads of buildings, including the Golden Gate Bridge in shaky San Francisco. Their job is to stop the roadway smashing into the towers and bringing the whole lot down. (With any luck.)

• **Make it some sandwiches.** No, not the sort you get filled with cheese or tuna fish. These sandwiches are made from thick layers of rubber and steel. Fancy sinking your chops into one?

Fix the sandwiches to your building's foundations.
They'll hold it up and stop it shaking.

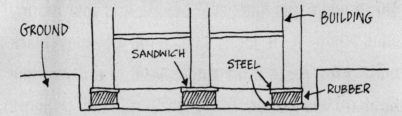

• **Weigh it down.** Some high-rise buildings have heavy weights at the top. You could call them top- heavy, ha! ha! The weights are worked electronically. When a quake hits, they rock in the opposite direction to the shaking. Balancing it out. Brilliant, eh? But horribly expensive. If you're short of cash, they're not for you.

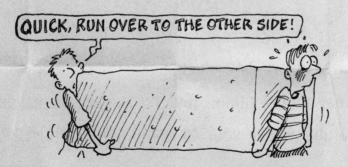

- **Put up some wallpaper.** That's right, wallpaper. But not the flowery stuff you get at your granny's. This is wallpaper like never before. And your granny would hate it. It looks like a roll of shiny black plastic. You paste it on and leave it to dry. Just like ordinary wallpaper. But there's nothing ordinary about this stuff. When it's dry, it's around three times harder than steel! That's seriously tough stuff. So instead of your wall cracking up, the seismic super-paper holds it all together.

- Clear out the garage. If you're thinking of building a garage under your house, think again. Large spaces like garages make the ground floor horribly unstable. If you've already got a garage, clear all the junk out (actually this bit's not essential but your parents will be pleased), then fix the garage to the foundations with giant springs. They'll bend with the shock, then ping back into place once the shaking's over. Leaving your house standing.

STAN'S HANDY HINTS NO.2

The best material to build with is something that gives, like wood or reinforced concrete (that's concrete strengthened with steel). Something that'll bend a bit. Don't use brittle bricks or hollow concrete blocks. They'll break if the quake's a big 'un. I'd also use shatter-resistant glass, if I were you.

LESSON 3: TESTING YOUR BUILDING

Right, it's crunch time. You've quake-proofed your house but will it stand up? Until it feels the full force of a real-life earthquake, you can't really tell. But a real-life earthquake's the last thing you want. So what on Earth do you do? Here's what the experts suggest:

1 First, build a model of your house. It doesn't need

to be exactly the same size. A scaled-down version will do.

2 Next, find a shake-table. No, a table with a wobbly leg won't do. This is a high-tech bit of equipment for testing out buildings in earthquake conditions. They're horribly expensive so you might need to borrow one from the experts.

3 Place your model on the table. Then make the table shake. (Note: you don't need to do the shaking yourself. A computer will do it for you. They're specially programmed to do just that.)

4 Stand back and watch what happens. If your house falls down, start again. (And this time, make sure you follow all the instructions.) If your house stays up, congratulations. You're obviously a whizz at seismic DIY.

STAN'S HANDY HINTS NO.3

It's a good idea to fix wardrobes and bookcases to the wall, so they don't fall on top of you during an earthquake. Fix latches on your kitchen cupboards. The last thing you want is flying tins of baked beans. If you can't find the fixings you need, try a company called Quake Busters in California. (Yes, it's a real company!) I've heard they'll fix anything.

LESSON 4: CHOOSING YOUR SITE

Be careful where you build your house. Some types of ground are shakier than others. Don't choose a spot where the ground's horribly soggy or soft. You'd be asking for trouble. When this type of soil's shaken up, the water in it rises to the surface, turning the soil to jelly. You won't get a building to stand up in that. I mean, have you ever tried standing a spoon in a bowl of wobbly jelly?

This is what happened to Mexico City in 1985. The city's built on a dried-out lake bed. A very bad move indeed. When the earthquake hit, the lake bed turned to jelly. Some buildings sank straight into the ground. Others tilted over on their sides. To make matters worse, the lake bed's shaped like a bowl. So what, you might ask? Well, the shape made the shock waves bigger and stronger. Which made the damage and devastation many, many times worse.

So what type of ground is best to build on? Somewhere nice and rock-solid would do.

STAN'S HANDY HINTS NO.4

Make sure you follow the local building code. Most quake-prone cities have one. Trouble is, quake-proofing's a seriously costly business. And some builders cut costs by breaking the rules. Instead of proper materials, they'll use cheaper, shoddier stuff, turning their buildings into killers. Besides, in poor countries, many people can't afford to live in posh, quake-proofed buildings. So they end up living in death-traps instead. It's a very tricky problem.

Shocking, isn't it? But it isn't all doom and gloom. All over the world, seismologists, architects and engineers are working hard to make shaky cities safer. Will they succeed? Who knows? The only way they can really put their new buildings to the test is to wait for the next earthquake. . .

A SHAKY FUTURE?

So is the future set to get shakier? Or will earthquakes soon be a thing of the past? Let's go back to our stressed-out seismologists and see what they have to say. Oh, dear, they're still squabbling. . .

If you think things have got off to a shaky start, watch out! They're set to get even shakier. The Big One could strike at any time. And, believe me, it'll be a megaquake. Where will it strike? Hard to tell. Chances are it'll be along a fault. A fault that's been nice and quiet for centuries. A fault where the strain's been building up and up, until suddenly it reaches breaking point. The Big One's already long overdue. Help! Help! Is there a table I can hide under?

Don't listen, it may never happen. Earthquakes aren't any more frequent than they used to be. It's just that more of them hit the headlines. And we scientists have got more sensitive seismographs so we can spot the small ones more easily. It might be ages before we can predict earthquakes accurately. If we ever can. But we're finding out lots more about them. So, even if we can't beat them just yet, we can learn to live with them. Pssst! You can come out from under the table now!

So you see, even the experts don't know for certain. But don't go digging up the playground just yet to see if your school's on shaky ground. (It won't get you out of double geography. Shame on you!) It's more likely your teacher will come down on you like a tonne of bricks for reading this book in class than you'll be shaken up by an earthquake. Of course with earthquakes you never know what shocks are in store, do you? You'll just have to wait and see. And that, I'm afraid, is the earth-shattering truth!